BIRDS OF THE NORTHERN ROCKIES

BIRDS of the NORTHERN ROCKIES

Tom J. Ulrich

MOUNTAIN PRESS PUBLISHING COMPANY
Missoula, 1984

Library of Congress Cataloging in Publication Data

Ulrich, Tom J.
  Birds of the northern Rockies

  Bibliography: p.
  Includes index.
  1. Birds — Rocky Mountains — Identification. I. Title.
QL683.R63U47   1984   598.2978   84-2048
ISBN 0-87842-169-6

Dedicated to my mother, Dorothy Ulrich

Acknowledgments

The most enjoyable and easiest portion in the development of this guide took five years and hundreds of hours stalking and sitting in blinds working to capture on film the photos used. Still it was not enough, and many thanks need to go to photographer friends who supplied species I was not able to record. The credits for these are given in the text.

In addition, I would like to express my appreciation to three associates — Bert Gildart, Dave Erickson, and Jan Wassink — for having read and commented editorially on the manuscript. I would also like to thank Mary Moe for amending my punctuation and grammar, and also Liz Tryon and Marsha Grimes for their moral support.

I also thank Clyde Lockwood, Chief Naturalist of Glacier National Park, and the Glacier National History Association. Their support was instrumental in the publication of this book.

Table of Contents

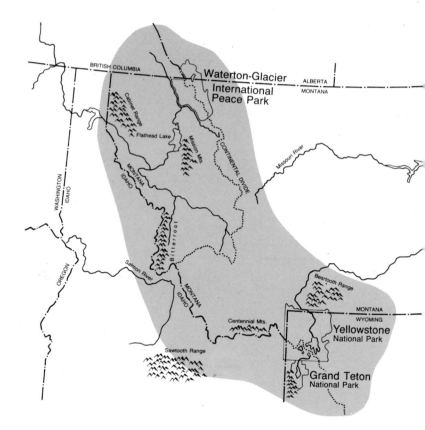

BRITISH COLUMBIA

Waterton-Glacier
International
Peace Park

ALBERTA
MONTANA

Cabinet Range

Flathead Lake

Mission Mts.

CONTINENTAL DIVIDE

Missouri River

WASHINGTON
IDAHO

MONTANA
IDAHO

Bitterroot

Salmon River

OREGON

MONTANA
IDAHO

Centennial Mts.

Beartooth Range

MONTANA
WYOMING

Yellowstone
National Park

Sawtooth Range

Grand Teton
National Park

Northern Rockies

Centrally located between the Colorado and Canadian Rockies, the total area of the Northern Rockies exceeds 100,000 square miles. Its valley floors average 3000 feet in elevation with many of the higher peaks exceeding 11,000 feet. The variety of avian fauna is as diverse as the vegetative zones which carpet all elevations. Some 12 designated National Wildlife Refuges, such as Red Rock and Ninepipes, are important stopovers for migrating waterfowl. Higher elevations which pose a beneficial habitat are such protected areas as Glacier-Waterton International Peace Park and Yellowstone National Park. There are no fewer than a dozen wilderness areas such as the Bob Marshall, Great Bear, Selway-Bitterroot, and Cabinet, preserving thousands of acres for excellent bird habitat.

Introduction

The purpose of this book is to provide a field guide of full-color photographs for persons interested in birds of the Northern Rockies and who would like to know them better. It is the result of several years effort to capture on film as many birds as can be found casually, regularly, or permanently in this region.

For the Northern Rockies, *Montana Bird Distribution* by Palmar David Skaar and a 1983 Checklist of Glacier National Park Birds indicate just over 230 species of birds recorded on a regular basis. The number would be somewhat higher if all incidental or rarity sightings were included. This book covers 170 species illustrated in full color. With few exceptions, the order of families is arranged in the sequence of the *Checklist of North American Birds*, sixth edition, published by the American Ornithologists' Union in 1983. It is hoped that the convenient size and flexible format serve as a useful field guide to the hiker, traveler, or kitchen window bird watcher.

Common Names

As a youngster in the Midwest, I took much of the avian fauna for granted, but one bold ruffian I became familiar with was the blue jay. The way these birds would flock to a feeding station almost brought on a feeling of hatred. After moving out West several years ago, I was surprised to hear the local people talk of an audacious "blue jay" harassing smaller birds for seed at the feeder. From my field guide I learned it was a Steller's jay, but every time I heard "blue jay" a picture of the eastern species crossed my mind.

The point is that vernacular names for a creature present many problems. They vary in different areas of the country and, occasionaly, the same name may be applied to several unrelated animals. This problem was recognized centuries ago when a Swedish botanist, Carol von Linne, devised the "Binomial System of Nomenclature." Using Latin, since it was the universal language at that time, a generic and specific name were given to every living creature on earth. To alleviate the problem in this book, one or more of the common names has been included along with the present scientific title.

Observing Birds

It was easy to ascertain her excitement as she hurriedly flipped through the pages of a bird field guide. So direct were her thoughts in looking for some visual clue, she was oblivious to my approach. Being the avid "birder," my growing curiosity as to what identification she was seeking got the better of me. Upon inquiring, the bird in question was kind of brown with a short bill and what she thought was cream-colored on the breast. We finally narrowed it to some 14 different possibilities.

The problem of trying to identify an unknown bird can be very frustrating. It is true such general characteristics as size and color help and could be a starting point, but you must learn to focus your attention on more detailed features. To accomplish this, binoculars or a spotting scope will enable you to observe such special field markings as eye, wing, and tail bars, rump patches, breast markings, bill shapes, head patterns, and eye rings.

Learning the correct terminology for these specific anatomical features will not only help focus your attention on the bird as you observe it, but will also be important for those birds you cannot immediately identify. These correct descriptive terms will allow the making of good field notes or the explaining of these terms to another well-versed person. After as many physical characteristics as possible are recorded in memory or on paper, try to recognize the bird's flight pattern, habitat, food preferences, and in general what the bird is doing, to expand the overall view of the subject.

As your knowledge about birds increases along with the ability to observe finer details, a whole new interesting world will open to you. Following are a few suggestions which should help add hours of enjoyment to this fast-growing activity:

- most birds are active from sunup to about 10:00 a.m.
- be prepared to walk some distance, thus enabling you to see more birds
- do not wear brightly colored clothing
- do not wear plastic type clothes, which are noisy
- walk slowly and quietly
- try to be alone or in small groups
- carry a field guide, such as this book
- frequent protected areas such as refuges, parks, or wildlife areas
- a notebook could be invaluable, especially after an exciting day of birding

400mm LENS WITH EXTENSION TUBE

Photographing Birds

Sitting in the total darkness of an early spring morning, the chill envelopes me as my eyes are closed for a lack of anything to focus on. As I try to concentrate on listening, many questions flash through my mind: am I too close? Too far? Will there be good light? Will anything show up? From previous investigations for tracks and droppings, I conclude right here, which seems the middle of nowhere, is the best location to sit in the cramped quarters of my blind. My goal is to capture on film the courtship ritual of the male sage grouse. Early each spring the males gather on ceremonial pieces of ground called "leks" and display for the females. Cocks arrive in total darkness before any sign of light and fill the crisp air with bubbling sounds from their frontal air sacs. In eager curiosity, I peek through a hole in my blind and can just barely see their dim images. When the sun finally hits the horizon, I realize dozens of proud courting male sage grouse surround my blind. The photographic opportunities are immense as all the cold, pain, and loneliness are forgotten.

For me, the greatest challenge of photographing birds is being able to penetrate my subjects' flight (or fright) distance. In walking toward a bird, chances are you will not get very close. When the bird takes flight, you have just penetrated its personal distance. Taking the human shape away has remarkable results. To accomplish this, I use several different types of blinds, but before I elaborate on these, a very important factor, always considered, is to keep the welfare of my subject a priority. Great care must be exercised, particularly when working a nest. Abandonment by the adults would wipe out the nest; this is especially true for larger birds like hawks, owls, and eagles.

Most of my time spent sitting in a blind is in one made of burlap and conduit which takes the shape of a teepee. It is inexpensive and easily set up. Holes can readily be cut to allow photographing at any level. Because of the teepee shape, one drawback is in not permitting me to shoot standing up, but rarely do I find this a problem.

This blind is a stationary position, too awkward for use in approaching a bird. Therefore, the photographer must devise ways to draw the subject to the blind. Using natural appearing bird feeders and bird baths will attract many species into very close range. Tantalizing morsels such as sunflower seeds, thistle seeds, cracked corn, peanuts, or beef suet will increase the variety of avian visitors even more.

A blind I have much fun with and use for most of my waterfowl photography is a muskrat hut blind. Made of chicken wire woven with cattails, it sits on a rubber inner tube. By wearing a pair of chest waders, I can move freely for hours, almost totally ignored to the extent of having birds alight on top of the blind.

Once I have devised a way to get close, camera equipment is of next importance to record my subject. A standard 35mm single lens reflex camera will suffice, especially with the wide range of lenses on the market. I mostly use a 400mm lens with 27mm of extension tube. The minimum focusing distance for this 400mm lens is 14 feet. Twenty-seven millimeters of extension tube allows me to focus at eight or nine feet with no loss of quality. Although it does shallow my depth of field and causes the loss of one f-stop, the ability to get 33% closer is most beneficial.

Preparations and equipment are a necessity, but are not the only requirements for capturing a bird on film. Often I have sat in a blind for hours over several days before photographing a bird to my satisfaction. The time spent waiting amplifies the virtue of patience, and only when all factors come together and gel will the rewards be harvested.

For the best success I find the following suggestions helpful.

- try to photograph on the level of your subject
- use a sturdy tripod
- use Kodachrome film for finer grain and exaggeration of warm colors
- watch for distracting objects in the background
- try to avoid harsh shadows and high contrast
- focus on the eye of your subject
- make sure the head of the subject is looking out of the photograph toward you
- although using artificial feeders, try to make them appear as natural as possible

Muskrat hut blind
Burlap teepee blind (on sage grouse lek)

Common Loon
Gavia immer

On isolated lakes or rivers of the spruce forest zone, it is common to hear springtime echoing calls of the loon. This wild loud laughter, so hard to forget, makes you realize you have returned to the wilderness. Unlike other birds, which have hollow bones, those of the loon are more solid. Additionally, loons have a dense waterproof plumage, long narrow wings, and large webbed feet located far back on the body. The result is a body shaped like a torpedo. When it comes to aquatics, the loon is unsurpassed. It possesses an ability to outmaneuver many species of fish. But on land, it is a different story. Standing erect, a loon can just barely waddle along. When hurried, it will drop down onto its breast where it flounders forward, using both wings and feet as aids for locomotion. Not very gregarious, they use the same body of water to nest year after year, and seldom will you see more than one pair per lake.

Western Grebe
Aechmophorus occidentalis

The western grebe is widely known for its spectacular courtship displays. Early stages find bits of nest material passed from bill to bill establishing the mating bond. As courtships heighten, pairs patter side by side over the water's surface on rapidly moving feet. Their bodies remain in an upright position with heads held horizontally. These rituals culminate with a plunge below the surface. Bulrush bordering sloughs can accommodate a whole nesting colony. Males gather nesting vegetation while females put it in place. Both adults incubate and, as with other grebes, young are carried on the parent's back hidden by the wing-coverts. The western grebe does not take well to human intrusion; consequently, nesting habitat is dwindling at a fast rate.

Eared Grebe
Podiceps nigricollis

Eared grebes are very gregarious diving birds which nest only a few feet apart. Many of these birds build their floating nests on reed-bordered shallow sloughs. Occasionally, birds arriving to incubate will rock these unstable platforms, so shallow and fragile in construction, often threatening to spill out an egg or two. If disturbed, incubating birds slip off their nests and disappear underwater, showing up moments later out on the lake in a protesting mood. With danger over, they return submerged to the nest. Young remain on the nest until all are hatched and then leave with the adults, never to return.

18

Common Loon 24"
Western Grebe 18"

Eared Grebe 9"

Red-necked Grebe

Podiceps grisegena

Unlike most grebes which colonize when breeding, the red-neck is distinctly a lover of solitude. After the courtship rituals of presenting bits of nesting material and "dancing" in unison across the surface of the water with bodies held upright, they manage to find a secluded spot in the reeds to hide their nest. Both sexes incubate on the damp floating nest of vegetation. Hatched young will often climb upon the parents' backs while waiting for their brothers and sisters to hatch out. Once incubation is complete, all leave the nest, never to return. Often the young can be seen riding on the back of an adult even as they dive during feeding. Marked with black crown, the white cheeks and explicit red neck easily identify this bird.

Pied-billed Grebe

Podilymbus podiceps

With names such as "helldiver," "dadchick," and "waterwitch," the pied-billed is our most common of grebes. These names developed from its ability to disappear almost instantly below the surface when disturbed. By compressing its feathers and changing its specific gravity, this grebe can sink until only the head remains above the surface. Equipped with lobed toes and feet far to the rear of its body, it easily catches tadpoles, shrimp, aquatic insects, or fish by swimming underwater. Nests are constructed of matted floating vegetation. Sufficient material is used so when the adult leaves it can pull the edges over to cover the eggs. Hatched nestlings often ride the back of adults. They remain there even while their parents dive to feed.

Red-necked Grebe 13"
Red-necked Grebe & young

T. ULRICH
T. ULRICH

Pied-billed Grebe 9"

K. FINK

White Pelican   *Pelecanus erythrorhynchos*

Most persons are astonished to find there are pelicans in the Northern Rockies, let alone that they nest here. These great white birds breed on islands in our western lakes. With some 30 days for incubation, these birds and their altricial young are vulnerable to avian and mammalian predators for almost three months. Featherless young, resembling plucked chickens, feed on regurgitated "soup" in their parents' pouches. As they get older, young reach down into the gullet of their parents for predigested fish. Eventually, the young outweigh their parents but lose this "baby fat" as they learn to fly. Feeding is executed in groups of pelicans swimming abreast, swinging their long bills from side to side through the water. This activity "herds" insects, crustaceans, amphibians, and fish before them, eventually to be scooped into the pouch.

Double Crested Cormorant   *Phalacrocorax auritus*

Home for the cormorant can be an island, cliff, dead snag, or bulrushes of a swamp. One thing's for certain: good fishing will be nearby. Here, this persistent deepwater diver captures fish and other small aquatic animals by direct pursuit. Less bouyant, cormorants swim low in the water with heads held high and bills slanted upward. Often they can be observed perched on a rock promontory, body upright, neck forming an S, and wings outstretched, drying in the wind. When taking off from water considerable feet pattering along the surface accompanied by a vigorous beating of the wings is imperative to become airborne. A good head wind is helpful. In flight, the rhythm slows to strong, heavy wing strokes with occasional intervals of gliding. Orientals often use this bird's expertise in fishing. With a loose rope tied around the neck, cormorants are allowed to dive and catch fish. Pulled from the water after a short period, fish are squeezed from the neck.

White Pelican 50"   T. ULRICH
Double Crested Cormorant 27" T. ULRICH

White Pelican flying   T. ULRICH
Double Crested Cormorant   T. ULRICH

Trumpeter Swan

Cygnus buccinator

On the verge of extinction just a half a century ago, the Migratory Bird Treaty Act was almost too late for the trumpeter. In the lower United States the population was reduced to an estimated 66. Creation of Red Rock Lake National Wildlife Refuge in southwest Montana helped to restore their numbers. Today they have increased to several hundred nesting pairs in that area alone. Trumpeters prefer to build their large nests on muskrat lodges or on islands they construct from bulrush. Sitting atop their rather conspicuous nests, the snow-white appearance of these swans contrasts sharply with their black bills. Often, their heads will be yellowed — the result of sticking them into the brackish water of some ponds. Trumpeters are distinguished from whistling swans *(Cygnus columbianus)* by the lack of a yellow mark on their bill.

Trumpeter Swan 45"
Whistling Swan 36"

T. ULRICH
B. STEVENS

Whistling Swan

D. ON

Canada Goose
Branta canadensis

Commonly known as "honkers," these rather brownish-bodied geese have black heads and necks, and distinct white cheeks. Very gregarious, except during nesting season, they are most often seen in their strung-out Vs during migration or on the feeding grounds. Extremely wary at the approach of an intruder, Canada geese raise their long necks and honk in low tones. If approached too closely, a short run, some powerful wing strokes, and a blast of honking will precede their taking flight. There are some 10 recognized subspecies of Canadas, which differ greatly in size and slightly in color. Before fall migration, adults molt their flying feathers simultaneously, thus becoming grounded for a few weeks.

Snow Goose
Chen caerulescens

A winter resident here, the snow goose is a northerly breeder which nests near the Arctic coast. Arriving here at the end of their fall migration, they can be seen settling like white clouds on the golden stubble of harvested fields. Wandering over the ground in broken array, plucking from side to side with a quick tweak of the bill and jerk of the neck, they graze their favorite grasses. On land or on the water, they also dig for bulbous roots. With the exception of black primaries and pink bills, these geese are as white as freshly fallen snow. Recently, the snow and blue geese have been classified as the same species and are now considered as color variants.

Pintail
Anas acuta

Occasionally, frozen ponds greet this early migrant on its way north in the spring. The grassy sloughs, ponds, marshes, and reedy shallows of larger lakes become excellent feeding areas for the pintail. While dabbling or tipping, their long necks enable them to reach down a little deeper. Females nest in nearby meadows or fields, usually in dry grass or a clump of weeds. Successful hatches must make the hazardous journey to water and will hopefully grow to stretch their wings, enabling flights to neighboring feeding areas. When it comes to protecting their brood, female pintails are among the most courageous of all ducks. There is little trouble in identifying drakes in flight by their long tails and slender necks.

26

Canada Goose 24"
Snow Goose 19"

Pintail 18½"

Mallard   *Anas platyrhynchos*

The mallard is a wild ancestor to the green-headed drakes found around most barnyards and city parks. With its wide range, high population density, and high tolerance for human activity, the mallard is perhaps our best-known duck. The iridescent green head, which can have a purplish gloss under certain light conditions, is abruptly separated from the chestnut breast by a white ring. After mating, these beautiful colors will give way to eclipse plumage, making him less than an object of beauty. The brown female incubates and raises her young unassisted. Any danger to her offspring generates a strong maternal display of flapping, splashing and quacking with total disregard for her own safety. Feeding is accomplished principally by dabbling shallow waters of sloughs, ponds, lakes, or rivers for aquatic vegetation, but a mallard is also partial to the cultivated grains of stubble fields. Interestingly, a mallard can cross freely with other species, such as Gadwall, pintail, and green-winged teal, but the offspring are usually sterile.

American Widgeon   *Anas americana*

Widgeon, baldplate, bluebill, poacher, are all names for a high-strung, diminutive duck that breeds almost exclusively in North America. A prominent white forehead and crown are direct cause for one of its common names, but "poacher" is derived from its fondness for wild celery. As other diving ducks surface with this prize, the thieving widgeon is ready and waiting to snatch away the desired item. When feeding for themselves, they swirl frequently, creating a tornado-like effect which sucks up aquatic vegetable matter from the bottom. They will also visit surrounding grain fields where, grazing like geese, they fatten on wheat and barley. Their walking ability, furthermore, allows the female to nest on upland prairies, since she can lead her ducklings to the water.

Male Mallard 16"
Female Mallard 16"

J. WASSINK
T. ULRICH

American Widgeon 13½"

Blue-winged Teal
Anas discors

A large white crescent immediately behind its bill will distinguish this teal from all others. This common visitor of the inland marshes, ponds, and sloughs waits until spring is well-advanced before making its journey northward. Early arrivals are usually those that wintered further north because the greatest percentage of bluewings are migrating from as far south as South America. A strict surface feeder, the blue-wing frequents the shallow edges close to shore, feeding on aquatic vegetation.

Green-winged Teal
Anas crecca

The green-winged teal is our smallest duck. It is also one of the earliest arrivals in spring. Habituating the inland sloughs, marshes, and streams, it feeds by dabbling to sift smaller invertebrates from the muddy bottom. Its diet also consists of various aquatic weeds that grow there. The female green-wing picks her nesting site well back from water; sometimes it is located near the edge of a meadow or forest. Very prolific, a brood may contain as many as 18 nestlings, but the usual number is 10 to 12.

Cinnamon Teal
Anas cyanoptera

Found mostly on the western side of the Continental Divide, this red teal prefers cattail or bulrush-bordered shallow edges of lakes and marshes. Here it finds adequate cover and an ample food supply it can dabble for from the surface. Not far from the shoreline, the inconspicuous female will utilize some heavy grass to conceal her nest. She is practically indistinguishable from a female blue-wing teal and oftentimes each will be mislabeled. The ducks themselves know the difference and crosses between the two species are unknown.

Male Blue-winged Teal 11"
Male Green-winged Teal 10½"

T. ULRICH
J. WASSINK

Male Cinnamon Teal 11"

T. ULRICH

Wood Duck
Aix sponsa

This incidental species is recognized by the brilliance of the male plumage. Sitting on a log in a patch of spring sunshine, the male wood duck's metallic sheen of blue, green, and purple reflected from his head contrasts sharply with its deep reddish-brown breast. Its preferred habitat is as unique as the colorful display of plumage. Woodland swamps, flooded bottomlands, and wood-fringed sloughs and streams are favorite retreats of the wood duck. Here, occasional dead and decaying trees provide nesting cavities. The site is usually near or over water and possibly as high as 30 feet. Most of the food eaten by a wood duck consists of vegetable matter, and if present, its favorite item is acorns. Because of logging, draining of woodland swamps, and hunting, this bird was almost eliminated. A 1918 law placed the wood duck under protection and a program of nest box building enabled it to recover to stable numbers.

Northern Shoveler
Anas clypeata

Scooping up mucky slough water with their broad-ended bills, shovelers sift the mouthfuls for small plants and animals which form their food. Comb-like teeth or "lanellae" line the outer edges of both upper and lower mandibles, straining out tiny food particles from the water and silt. The tongue and roof of the mouth are very sensitive and determine what is eaten. Except for this oversized bill, "spoonbill" closely resembles a blue-wing teal in appearance, flight, and habits. Brownish sides with white breast and white under the tail provide a good method of identification. Males, however, molt early and often appear similar to females. Females rear the young which, when hatched, have bills no larger than those of other ducklings. About ten days later the unmistakable spatula-like bill has developed.

Male Wood Duck 13½"   T. ULRICH
Female Wood Duck   T. ULRICH

Male Shoveler 14"   T. ULRICH

Redhead
Aythya americana

Closely resembling a canvasback, it takes a conditioned eye to distinguish the redhead. Both frequent the same type of habitat and display similar behavior patterns. The male redhead can be distinguished from a male canvasback by a high forehead, darker gray back, and shorter neck. The uniformly brown female, with dark-tipped bill has a questionable habit of depositing her eggs in other birds' nests. Communal "dump nests" are common between two or more redheads, but can also include eggs from another species. All hatchings will be reared by the incubating female, resulting in clutches of fifteen or more young.

Canvasback
Aythya valisineria

The scientific name, *valisineria*, refers to any aquatic plant commonly called wild celery. Being an important part of a canvasback's diet, the species name of this waterfowl was derived from it. Preferring the soft white roots of this plant, canvasbacks will dive to 30 feet in quest of the succulent prize. When feeding on wild celery, this duck is often accompanied by other species of waterfowl. Redhead, widgeon, and scaup also appreciate this same food and will attempt to steal some as the canvasback breaks surface with a bill full of choice roots. When not feeding, the canvasback will rest toward the center of our large lakes and reservoirs. Nesting territories are generally sloughs or ponds near the lakes and here a female will conceal a weaved nest of plant material.

Male & Female Redhead 14½"
Male Canvasback 15"

Female Canvasback

Harlequin Duck

Histrionicus histrionicus

The cold water of Rocky Mountain streams and lakes is the summer home of the beautiful harlequin duck. Strange as it may seem, the harlequin is a diving sea duck that migrates inland to court, mate, and produce its offspring on swift glacial fed streams. Here it has no trouble diving under the strongest of currents to feed on small fish or insect larva. The decorated pattern and elegant form of the male is not easily mistaken. His slate-blue color, imprinted with many white markings and reddish sides, differs greatly from the brownish female. She has three facial white spots. It is easy to understand why these stately birds are called "lords and ladies" of the waters.

Ring-necked Duck

Aythya collaris

From a distance, the light ring on the bluish bill of a ring-necked duck can be seen; but you have to be fairly close to observe the brown neck band which identifies the drake. This ring near the tip of the bill gives this duck the more common colloquial name "ringbill." The general overall appearance of a ring-neck is different from that of a lesser scaup, which has a darker back and grayer flanks. These species are frequently seen together and have similar habits. The ring-neck is a much deeper diver, up to 40 feet, but its most common way of feeding is dabbling in shallow water for pondweed or bulrush tubers.

Male Harlequin Duck 12" T. ULRICH
Female Harlequin Duck T. ULRICH

Ring-necked Duck 12" T. ULRICH

Lesser Scaup
Aythya affinis

The lesser scaup is a true diving duck and prefers lakes where pondweeds grow near the surface. When not feeding, this scaup spends much of its time far out on larger lakes and reservoirs, loafing, its bill tucked under a wing. A very close relative, the greater scaup, *(Aythya marila)* may occasionally be observed as a transient, but it breeds further north and inhabits our coastal flyways. Diagnostically, the greater has more of an iridescent green head and darker back. The brown lesser female has a conspicuous white crescent-shaped area over her bill. She is a rather late nester and usually locates the nest, a small depression in the ground lined with grass and down, close to water.

Barrow's Goldeneye
Bucephala islandica

Small isolated mountain lakes where forests crowd the water's edge make excellent summer homes for Barrow's goldeneye. Another colloquial name, Rocky Mountain goldeneye, indicates how abundant these birds are in this area. By mid-April, each small lake owns a courting flock of goldeneyes. With heads puffed out to their greatest possible extent, males swim bowing toward a receptive female. Frequently, these same males give a backward kick, strong enough to send a jet of water skyward, only to go on feeding patiently. At any time the flock may suddenly take off and circle the lake several times, eventually to splash down and resume courting. This species is a tree-nester using cavities in decaying trunks close to the water. Probing the shallows, these goldeneyes feed on aquatic insects and crustaceans.

Common Goldeneye
Bucephala clangula

Because of a peculiar penetrating whistle made by its wings in flight, the goldeneye is often called "whistler." This sound is one of the earliest to be heard in spring as they return to their nesting territories of woodland lakes and streams. Here the female looks for an old hollow snag or a cavity in a tree to nest. The courtship of the male is elegantly handled while swimming around the female. All head feathers erect, he thrusts his neck so his bill is pointed straight up. With the back of his head touching his rump, he emits a harsh rasping note and kicks forward to display his orange legs behind him.

Lesser Scaup 12"
Burrow's Goldeneye 13"

Common Goldeneye 13"

Bufflehead
Bucephala albeola

The original name for this bird was "buffalo headed," a reference to its oversized head. It was later shortened to its present title. When viewed from a distance, the small drake appears almost snow white; closer observation reveals a black and white pattern. Swimming nearby may be a brownish-colored female, distinguished by an elongated white patch behind and below her eye. If nesting, she uses an available flicker hole close to shoreline. Getting through the three-inch opening is tight, but this is where she will incubate her eggs. After hatching, the downy young jump from the entrance and are led to water by their mother. Endowed with natural swimming and diving abilities, the ducklings are taught by the female what to catch as food. At seven weeks, the young can fly and will venture from the home pond.

Ruddy Duck
Oxyura jamaicensis

With some 60 colloquial names drawn from many aspects of its body and behavior patterns, the ruddy duck's generic name *Oxyura*, meaning sharp tail, is noteworthy. When it is elevated over the body, almost touching the back of his head, this tail is an important part of courtship. When the motion is combined with a rapid stretching up and down of his neck and a tapping of his bill to his puffed chest, this boastful suitor is sure to entice a captivating female. Her basket-like nest is constructed above water and composed of materials from surrounding vegetation. Surprisingly, her eggs are enormous and exceed those of a mallard or canvasback. An average clutch will weigh three pounds, some three times her own weight. Diving for aquatic vegetation is the main food source for the ruddy duck, but because of the positioning of the feet for diving, neither sex can walk on land.

Male Bufflehead 10"
Female Bufflehead

T. ULRICH

Male Ruddy displaying for Female 11"

T. ULRICH

Gadwall

Anas strepera

When it comes to colors, one duck has to be the least decorated and a drake gadwall surely fits the bill. Often called "gray duck," striking colors are absent from most of the body, which is a slate color blended with shades of brown. The gadwall is a true puddle duck and prefers smaller marshy ponds or sloughs of the prairies. It does not take to deep water because it is mainly a surface feeder and likes to dabble for vegetation. Its ability to walk enables this duck to wander into adjacent grain fields and wooded areas in search of nuts, or it will often pick a nest site somewhat distant from water.

Hooded Merganser

Lophodytes cucullatus

The elegant headdress of a male hooded merganser can only be compared in beauty to that of a drake wood duck. Seen most of the time as a collapsed white stripe behind the eye, during courtship display these elongated hairlike feathers will elevate, becoming a flattened white crest. The female has a similar crest of elongated feathers on the back of her head, only these are reddish brown in color — hers may be fanned at any time and for no apparent reason. Being a cavity nester, she will often compete with wood ducks or goldeneyes for possession of a nest. Interestingly, the eggs of two species are often found in the same nest being incubated by both ducks in turns. This conflict arises from the destruction of natural habitat near water. Frequently, the young must travel half a mile to water after hatching. On water, they swim and dive freely after aquatic fauna, which comprise most of their diet.

Male Gadwall Duck 14½"   K. FINK
Male Hooded Merganser 13"   T. ULRICH

Female Hooded Merganser 13"   T. ULRICH

Common Merganser

Mergus merganser

Built somewhat like a loon, the exceptional diving abilities of the "razor bill" are so good that few fish can escape it. It captures both beneficial and trash fish by direct pursuit underwater. Insects and crustaceans supplement the carnivorous diet of this waterfowl. When one surfaces with a fish, others close at hand will set upon that merganser in an attempt to steal the prize. For this reason, much of what they eat is swallowed whole and always head first. When the young jump from the cavity nest for the first time, they are already endowed with diving abilities. Any threat or danger will keep the ducklings close to their mother's heels as she dives and swims underwater. A close cousin, the red-breasted merganser *(Mergus serrator)* is rarely seen in this area and tends to be a more northern bird. The red-breasted lacks the distinctive separation of a brown neck and a white breast.

Male Common Merganser 18"
Female Common Merganser

Red-breasted Merganser 16"

Turkey Vulture   *Cathartes aura*

Although the feeding habits of the vulture are repulsive to some people, it does play an important role in the disposal of decomposing animal matter. Sufficiently adapted for scavenging with a hooked beak, it also uses keen eyesight and the sense of smell while riding thermals for hours watching for carrion. This avian scavenger is easily identified from below when soaring. The under surface of the wings are brown with gray along the trailing edge. From eye level it can further be identified by a red, feather less head. A gregarious species, individuals often join others in the eve ning where they roost in groups until the sun is well up. In these early rays they spread their wings for drying. Moments later they catch the first rising thermals. They are often referred to as a "buzzard," but this is a misnomer, for true buzzards are actually hawks. Nevertheless, this term is rather deep-rooted and will probably never be replaced.

Red-tailed Hawk   *Buteo jamaicensis*

"Chicken hawk," is a name wrongly attributed to this bird. It is blamed for something other species of hawks do, but in reality very little of a red tailed hawk's diet consists of poultry. What domestic fowl they do take is easily outweighed by the number of smaller mammalian varmints they eliminate. Hunting is accomplished by soaring, or by perching high in a tree where the red-tail can survey the surrounding terrain for the slight est movement of unsuspecting prey. They prefer forest margins, as their wide wingspan is not that well adapted for quick maneuvering in deep woods. A mass of twigs at considerable height, usually occupied the previous year, serves as the nest for this bird of prey.

Swainson's Hawk   *Buteo swainsoni*

This hawk is a common buteo of open prairies and grasslands. Named after a nineteenth-century ornithologist, William Swainson, the hawk often pursues a method of hunting similar to a harrier (marsh hawk). Gliding back and forth, low over the prairie, it will at any moment make a sudden pounce on some unsuspecting creature. Farmers fancy this pre dator, as it rarely attacks poultry or game birds, but concentrates on insect and mammalian vermin. Food is abundant on the plains, but any poison or pesticides are transmitted to them, their reproductive ability, or to their young. Late nesters, their crude stick nests in bushes or trees could also be cohabited in the lower levels by doves, house sparrows, or finches.

Vulture 25"
Red-tailed Hawk 18"
T. ULRICH
J. GEORGE

Vulture drying wings
Swainson's Hawk 18"
T. ULRICH
A. NELSON

Ferruginous Hawk   *Buteo regalis*

Squirrel-hawk is an apt name for this large, regal monarch of our shortgrass prairies and badlands where ground squirrels abound. Often seen in its common light phase, a ferruginous can be identified by reddish-gray color above varying to almost white below. Hunting tactics include both soaring at high elevations or perching on some high promontory to watch for prey. Other small mammals, such as prairie dogs and several species of mice, combined with occasional snakes and birds, round out this species' carnivorous diet. Indiscriminate poisoning of rodents by range owners has had a direct effect on this buteo. Poison-tainted prey, eaten by adults or carried back for their young, has taken a dramatic toll.

Marsh Hawk   *Circus cyaneus*

The marsh hawk is our only representaive of an Old World group known as harriers. They feed mainly by flying low with wings held in a shallow V, their white rump and slender tail trailing behind. Skimming the weed tops of open marshes or meadows, the harrier's keen eyesight and very acute hearing enables it to detect the small mammals, frogs, and insects that make up a varied diet. A sudden stop drops the hawk with open talons to catch its prey; if not feeding young, he devours it immediately. Frequently, a male will carry prey to its incubating mate and when overhead, will drop the victim to the female, who rises from the nest to make a mid-air catch. Females are slightly larger and generally brown in color while males are gray with black wing tips.

American Kestrel (Sparrow Hawk)   *Falco sparverius*

The small and handsome sparrow hawk is misnamed and leads many to conclude it feeds on sparrows, which it rarely does. For this reason it has been given another name, the American kestrel, indicating a relationship to the European kestrel. This name is preferred since insects and mice are its staples. Sitting on all kinds of conspicuous perches, such as telephone poles and wires, fence posts, or dead tree trunks, it keeps an open eye for prey. Nicknamed "windhoverer," it sometimes hunts by remaining stationary in the air. Rapidly beating its wings, with a fanned-out tail, it scans the ground for an encouraging movement. When nesting, it prefers to use cavities, often choosing old abandoned holes of flickers and other woodpeckers. Its small size; upper parts red-to-cinnamon, and back barred with black will easily identify this New World falcon.

Hawkowl   *Surnia ulula*

Seen as a rare visitor to our area, this aptly-named avian predator blends the habits and appearance of both hawks and owls. The quick wing beats it uses to attain considerable speed, its long tail, and its trim body are very suggestive of a hawk, yet its soundless flight, large head, soft feathers, and large yellow eyes label it as a true owl. Perched atop a dead stump, surveying for any prey that scurries about below, a hawkowl can be approached quite closely. This absence of fear is probably due to its lack of familiarity with human beings.

Ferruginous Hawk 20"   A. NELSON
American Kestrel 8½"   T. ULRICH

Marsh Hawk 16½"   T. ULRICH
Hawkowl 14"   D. ON

Osprey
Pandion haliaetus

Living entirely on a diet of fish, the osprey is usually not to be found far from sizable bodies of water. Since this "fish hawk" is not a deep diver, it catches fish on or near the surface, or in rather shallow water. Hovering over its prey momentarily, it suddenly plunges downward like a spearhead to seize an unsuspecting fish with its outstretched talons. Then it beats its way back to a nest or feeding perch. Osprey are truly magnificent birds with their upper parts brown and crowns somewhat blackish. A black stripe passes through the eye and on down the side of the neck. Contrasting with this is a white neck and underparts.

Peregrine Falcon
Falco peregrinus

Unlike its relative the prairie falcon, which feeds mainly on ground-dwelling mammals, the peregrine kills only in flight. Shooting downward in a power dive on partially closed wings, the peregrine strikes the fleeing bird a lethal blow with its feet. Small birds are carried away, while larger ones are followed to the ground, plucked and torn to pieces before being carried to a nest or favorite perch. After fledging, families break up in search of suitable wintering territories. These wide-ensuing peregrinations are what give this majestic bird its name. It is discerned by the dark markings on its head, often described as "sideburns" or a "mustache."

Prairie Falcon
Falco mexicanus

Lacking the spectacular hunting techniques of a peregrine falcon, our smaller prairie falcon is somewhat faster in flight. The long pointed wings allow it to attain speeds in excess of 175 miles per hour, enabling it to overtake any prey. Much of what it eats are ground squirrels, other small rodents, and occasionally a bird. Since it prefers the western arid mesas, canyons, and cliffs, the prairie falcon is far more pale in appearance than a peregrine and also lacks the prominent "mustache." With habitat not influenced by human intrusion, it seems prairie falcon populations would stabilize, but this is not true. The squirrels and mice these birds subsist on contain such high levels of pesticides that successful hatchings and rearing of prairie falcon numbers are declining.

Osprey 22"
Peregrine Falcon 16"

Prairie Falcon 15"

Golden Eagle

Aquila chrysaetos

This eagle derives its common name from golden buff feathers on its head and neck. All other parts of this bird are a darker brown except for the lighter basal portion of the tail and the white wing patches that can be seen while flying. Occupying different habitat than its close relative, the bald eagle, there is little competition between them. Found mostly in higher mountains and open plains, the golden eagle does most of its hunting while in flight. In our Northern Rockies, Columbian ground squirrels constitute the greatest portion of its diet. This eagle uses cliffs, promontories, and crags as nesting sites, but also utilizes this habitat as a vantage point to watch for prey. It has taken the golden eagle millions of years to evolve its predatory perfection and reach the top of the food chain, thus making it sensitive to any changes in its habitat. Eagles and other predatory birds cannot change as fast as modern civilization sometimes demands them to. Traps, poisoned baits, herbicides, and insecticides are indiscriminate killers, and if the eagle is to survive, man must make the change.

Bald Eagle

Haliaeetus leucocephalus

The bald eagle should interest everyone by virtue of its status as our national emblem. Surprisingly, this regal bird is not as noteworthy when its behavior is taken into account. Although quite capable of killing its own prey, much of what it feeds on is carrion. Often found near water, especially larger lakes, rivers, and the sea, bald eagles will patrol for dead fish. They also feed on live fish close enough to the surface to be seized with their talons. Occasionally mammals, crippled ducks, and wild birds will supplement their diet or the diet of their young. Bald eagles generally have two offspring reared in a nest of tremendous size. The same site is used each year with an addition of new sticks trampled with new grass. Parents mate for life and share nest duties. Juvenile bald eagles have mottled brown and white plumage and fly at about thirteen weeks. It is not until four or five years later that these birds will acquire a white head and white tail.

Golden Eagle 32"   T. ULRICH
Immature Bald Eagle   T. ULRICH

Adult Bald Eagle 32"   T. ULRICH
Immature Bald Eagle   T. ULRICH

Spruce Grouse (Franklin's) *Dendragapus canadensis*

Spruce grouse is a fairly common, very tame grouse of coniferous forests. It is often labeled with the name "foolhen," because it is easy to approach. This subdued attitude has had a dramatic effect in decreasing the bird's populations. The sexes are noticeably different, with the best identifying characteristic being the well-defined black breast patch of the male. The male lacks any kind of a featherless area on the neck or colorful air sacs, like other grouse. During courtship, the male spruce grouse will fly to a branch and, while in flight, strike his wings together twice above his back producing a double clapping sound. He will also defend his territory with a handsome strutting pose.

Ruffed Grouse *Bonasa umbellus*

With the advance of spring, the male ruffed grouse seeks out its territory, an activity which usually includes one or more drumming stages. He performs this characteristic wing-beating display repeatedly in the same place, facing the same direction, and using the same "drumming log." At peak season he "drums" all day, but prior to and after this he will perform only during morning and evening. Standing erect, leaning on his tail, his cupped wings begin to beat the air, accelerating until they vanish into a blur, making the hollow thumping sound. As an inquisitive female arrives, he quickly assumes a strutting attitude. With tail fanned out, neck ruffs raised and wings drooping, he moves his neck in a rotary motion, making a hissing sound while rushing toward the female. Both sexes are predominately wood brown and crested, and have extensively barred tails and dark ruffs on the neck.

Spruce Grouse displaying 13"
Male Ruffed Grouse drumming 14"

L. KAISER
T. ULRICH

Ruffed Grouse

D. ON

Sage Grouse
Centrocercus urophasianus

On a cool spring morning, still in darkness, a male sage grouse takes his position on a strutting ground known as a "lek." Here he defends his territory, at the same time trying to perform an age-old courtship ritual. With a complex sequence of stepping, wing-brushing movements, and increasing inflations of his esophagus for expansion of the huge air sacs, the visual and audible sounds produced by this display allure receptive females. Territorialism is great as each male watches for crossed boundary lines. He may be distinguished from the female by a black throat and white breast feathers concealing two large areas of olive-skinned gular sacs.

Sharp-tailed Grouse
Tympanuchus phasianellus

Early spring, male sharp-tailed grouse gather on ceremonial areas of ground called "leks." Here they attract females for breeding. Both sexes are nearly identical in plumage except when the male courting dance begins. His inconspicuous yellow comb becomes enlarged, and paired violet air sacs on the neck become exposed. Otherwise, their overall dappled-buff coloration is contrasted with somewhat lighter underparts. Its colloquial name came about from the slightly elongated central tail feathers, which are perfectly erect while the male sharptail is displaying. Each male on the displaying grounds defends his own territory, while continually pushing toward the center. The few dominant males in the center will do most of the mating.

Male Sage Grouse 22" T. ULRICH
Male Sage Grouse with air bag expanded T. ULRICH

Male Sharp-tailed Grouse 15" T. ULRICH

Blue Grouse

Dendragapus obscurus

During spring and early summer a hollow, hooting sound emerges from the dense forest of the high mountains. Careful investigation will trace this sound to a male blue grouse displaying in his territory. With close observation, a red featherless neck skin fringed by the white downy bases of surrounding feathers becomes clearly visible. Most active early in the morning or evening, this showy display is used to entice a receptive female for mating. The blue grouse can be confused with a spruce grouse, as both inhabit the same range. To best distinguish the two, look for the male blue grouse's bluish-gray overall appearance or lack of a definite black breast patch.

Gray Partridge

Perdix perdix

Another naturalized citizen, the gray partridge was imported from Hungary to Alberta in 1908-09. The population increased so rapidly that a shooting season was opened in 1913. It does not compete with native species because it thrives in cultivated habitat. Very gregarious out of nesting season, coveys eat shoots, leaves, seeds, and waste grain. These birds provide excellent sport for the gamebird hunter by running fast, flying fast, and hiding well. During winter snows, they dig down to stubble, which provides both food and shelter from the wind.

Male Blue Grouse displaying 17"   T. ULRICH
Blue Grouse displaying   T. ULRICH

Gray Partridge 10"   A. NELSON

White-tailed Ptarmigan

Lagopus leucurus

Relying on protective coloration, the white-tailed ptarmigan is generally difficult to notice against a lichen-covered rocky backgrond. Summer plumage finds the adult male mottled-barred black, buff, and white on the back and white below. Females are similar, but tend to have a more yellowish color on their backs. Both sexes have a diagnostic white tail which stays white year round. As summer gives way to fall, darker feathers are replaced by white ones. By first snow, winter plumage is usually complete and the white-tailed ptarmigan is a pure white bird except for black bill and eyes. Occasionally, Mother Nature goes awry, and white birds can be found foraging on the still-fall foliage. Found above timberline year round feeding on buds and seeds, this seasonal change is imperative to its survival. This is illustrated when an avian predator flies overhead. Feeding ptarmigan will start to cluck and carry on. Soon, all will stop and sit down, their heads rolled to the side watching the sky above. Once the intruder is out of sight, the ptarmigan assume their normal feeding behavior. When startled, a bright red comb appears above their eyes.

Male White-tailed 10"　　T. ULRICH
Fall plumage　　T. ULRICH

Female White-tailed　　T. ULRICH
Winter Plumage　　T. ULRICH

Chukar

Alectoris chukar

Originally introduced from Asia, the chukar is doing so well that it is considered a North American game bird. This species prefers rugged, arid canyons which support sparse cover bunchgrass and sagebrush. Here it feeds primaily on leaves and seeds of weed plants. Water is important in these dry areas, especially during the breeding season. Summer rains for drinking or a source of succulent plants for water can be factors affecting offspring mortality. Broods vary in size, averaging eight. When several broods come together they form a covey, which is the important social unit of chukar partridge.

Ring-necked Pheasant

Phasianus colchicus

There are some sixty species and many subspecies of pheasants in almost all parts of the world. Many of these were introduced to North America late in the eighteenth century. The ring-necked pheasant of today is largely a composite, produced by the interbreeding of several strains, with the Eastern Chinese pheasant being the most dominant. This ringneck thrives best in open farm country where the climate is mild and snow not too deep or lasting. Here it will feed on grains, seeds, berries, grasshoppers, and insects. A casual traveler should see these birds along country roadways. When approached, a pheasant will sneak away through low cover or burst forth alarmingly on roaring wings, cackling noisily, to fly fast and low and usually land in more cover a short distance away.

Turkey

Meleagris gallopavo

At one time the turkey was nominated by Ben Franklin as our national symbol because it was strictly North American. The name turkey (meaning guinea fowl) was acquired from concurrent introduction of our species and the African guinea fowl to Europe about 1550. They called both of these imports "turkey" and today the misnomer continues. A permanent resident of oak woodlands and pine-oak forests of the East, the turkey has been introduced to various areas of our Northern Rockies. Foraging on the ground, this bird has adapted well in its food habits by shifting from acorns to pine nuts, berries, insects, tubers, and weed seeds. Each spring the polygamous male defends his territory or "strutting ground" and displays to attract eligible females. His naked bluish head with red wattles is accentuated by the bronze plumage, beard, and brown-rimmed fan-shaped tail feathers. While displaying, a long pencil-like "snood" hangs down over the bill, while at all other times it is short and erect.

Chukar 10"   T. ULRICH
Turkey Gobbling 34"   T. ULRICH

Ring-necked Pheasant 27"   T. ULRICH
Turkey displaying   T. ULRICH

Snowy Egret   *Egretta thula*

Since it nests in the southern United States, this egret is only seen as a
casual visitor to our area. Because of this, the fine recurved aigrettes and
plumes of courtship are never viewed. When feathers were fashionable,
great numbers of snowy egrets were destroyed, their plumes plucked. This
was disastrous because these plumes are carried during breeding season,
meaning the birds were killed on nesting grounds and any young were left
to die. Laws forbidding the sale of wild bird feathers curbed this slaughter.
This bird can be observed standing on a rock promontory waiting for prey
to come by, or standing in shallow water poking one leg up and down to stir
the bottom.

Black-crowned Night Heron   *Nycticorax nycticorax*

Feeding mainly in the evening and all through darkness, the black-
crowned is not strictly a nocturnal bird and can be observed moving about
during daytime. It has a different technique of feeding than other herons
— instead of standing motionless waiting for prey, the night heron is
constantly moving about in search of it. On short legs it wades the shallow
water or walks on tangled masses of vegetation looking for fish, frogs, or
insects. A warm sunny day can find this bird in idleness, perched on some
fence post or on the shore in its characteristic squat pose, with little of the
neck visible. Sunning perches and feeding grounds are located far from
nesting rookeries, which are situated in trees or in the rushes and cattails
surrounding a marsh. In flight, a characteristic "quok" sound has earned
it such labels as "squawk" and "quawk."

Great Blue Heron   *Ardea herodias*

The great blue heron is our largest of herons and generally inhabits the
isolated wetlands. It hunts by either of two methods. Remaining motionless for minutes — almost sleeplike in appearance — it suddenly shoots
out its dagger-like beak with incredible speed. An unwary frog or fish has
been impaled. It can also feed by stalking its prey. Taking each step slowly
as it lifts a foot above the surface and slides it below the water with hardly
a ripple, soon the victim is within striking distance. When startled, great
blue takes flight with slow wing strokes exposing a blue of the wings.
Simultaneously its neck is pulled back into an S with long legs stretched
behind. This bird often nests in rookeries among the highest tree tops, but
will also use shrubs of islands in our larger lakes.

Snowy Egret 20"   T. ULRICH
Great Blue Heron 38"   T. ULRICH

Black-crowned Night 20"   J. WASSINK
Young Great Blue Heron   T. ULRICH

American Bittern
Botaurus lentiginosus

Statue-like, with beak aimed skyward, the bitten's neck feathers blend with the reeds. If there is a breeze, this bird will sway like the surrounding vegetation. Eyes are positioned lower than normal, enabling it to watch any intruder. If approached too closely, it flaps awkwardly into the air, croaks, and flies off to a new location. Rarely would the bittern venture out to open water, yet, not confined to a marsh, it will take to large meadows or pastures where prey can be slowly stalked. Seeing a small mammal or some invertebrate, it thrusts its rapier-like beak forward to impale the inattentive creature. In spring, on its breeding grounds, the male bittern utters a series of two or three guttural notes. From these somewhat wooden or liquid sounds have come such local names as "thunder pump" or "slough pumper."

Sandhill Crane
Grus canadensis

The dance of the sandhill can be seen at any time of the year, but is most intense during breeding season. This bow and jump into the air with wings spread and legs dangling is one of the more remarkable performances in the natural world. As one starts, others join in to initiate the preliminary stages of pairing. Mates will then venture off to some inaccessible marsh or slough, spending the next three months there rearing their young. They feed on roots, insects, crustaceans, frogs, and mice until the young can fly. In early fall, the family units regroup and start their fall migration southward.

American Bittern 23"
Sandhill Cranes 37"

D. ON
T. ULRICH

Sandhill Crane

J. WASSINK

Virginia Rail
Rallus limicola

Very secretive, a Virginia rail creeps about the tangled stems of dead reeds and rushes which form a canopy over the water of most marshes. Its long toes find an easy foothold and allow free movement while feeding on insects, snails, and slugs in this fringe vegetation. Occasionally, a rail will come out on exposed mud, walking slowly and delicately with head moving back and forth, capturing insects with its long down-curved bill. Startled, it runs for cover with its body and neck stretched out and its tail straight up. Trying to approach a rail under its thick maze of cover is almost impossible. More often heard, especially during courtship, the male gives a series of loud metallic notes and this will indicate his general location.

Sora
Porzana carolina

About the size of a half-grown chicken, a sora will wade over the tangled vegetation of prairie sloughs or marshy shallows of lakes, investigating for insects, snails, and seeds. Very secretive, an observer might catch a glimpse of one darting across matted vegetation in a small opening of the reeds. Flushing a sora reveals a stocky body bordered with short wings and legs dangling as it flies, usually only a short distance before it drops again into the shelter of the reeds. On longer flights, (the sora's wintering grounds are as far south as Central America) the wing beats are much stronger as this bird fully extends its neck and legs.

American Coot
Fulica americana

Coots, or "mudhens," are the most common waterfowl congregating at farm ponds or any large standing body of water. Here they feed mainly by diving to the bottom for submerged vegetation. Another method of securing plant material is to "dabble" from the surface in a manner similar to that of ducks. Equipped with long, lobed toes, their feet are designed for swimming and walking over lily pads. When disturbed, a coot takes off by galloping over the water, simultaneously thrashing its wings and feet. The "mudhen" is easily identified by its dark slate body, white bill, and white under-tail markings. Occasionally, coots will anger waterfowl hunters by taking over feeding areas that would otherwise attract ducks.

Virginia Rail 7½"
Sora Rail 7"

D. ON
J. GEORGE

American Coot 12"

American Avocet

Recurvirostra americana

If someone's first encounter with an avocet is anywhere near its breeding grounds, it is probably going to be an alarming situation. Amidst the screaming cries there is little time to notice the cinnamon head or long curved bill, as the black and white body comes straight for your head. The avocet will turn quickly and sail past you at the last moment, avoiding impact. This attacking procedure is repeated over and over until retreat becomes first priority. Once the bird calms down and returns to normal activities, its unusual feeding habits can be viewed. As it sweeps from side to side, a long upcurved bill is used to skim the surface of the water for insects and larva. Pipestem blue legs (hence the occasional nickname "blue shanks") allow this bird to probe mud in deeper water for food. Several birds will stride together, screening the surface. They will also show this same togetherness during nesting season when several nests may share the same sandbar or island. Nests, located near water, are a simple depression in the sand, lined with grass and weed stems.

Black-necked Stilt

Himantopus mexicanus

Walking with extended and deliberate strides, the extremely long legs of this stilt are highly specialized for wading alkaline lakes and pools of the Great Basin. One can only admire the skillful, graceful way they wade in breast-deep water, searching for aquatic insects. When this stilt feeds on dry land, the legs are bent, bringing the body lower so the long neck and bill reach the ground for easy access to insect prey. When their territories are invaded, the excitement almost seems to make them tremble. Those immediately threatened collapse suddenly, as if one of their legs snapped in two, pantomiming a broken-leg act. Not a very common shorebird, the black-necked stilt is only viewed as a transient in the Northern Rockies.

American Avocet 15" T. ULRICH
American Avocet on nest T. ULRICH

Black-necked Stilt 13" D. ON

Semipalmated Plover

Charadrius semipalmatus

It is best to observe this little plover in spring while it's migrating north. Periodically it stops at local sloughs and the mud flats of marshes, where its presence serves as a pleasant reminder that spring is not far away. Contiuing its journey, it may fly as far north as the Arctic Circle, where it nests. August and September see the southward migration reinforced by a new generation. In flight they are very communal, but upon alighting will scatter out independently. They run a few steps, dart at some creature on the sand, then stand for several moments before another run. A short, thick bill is ill-adapted for probing mud, so feeding is conducted from the surface for aquatic insects. Partially webbed toes, from which its name semipalmatus was inspired, combined with a single black neck band, are the best identifying characteristics.

Killdeer

Charadrius vociferus

As the scientific title vociferus implies, the killdeer has a noisy repertoire of calls. Most noticeable is the repeated ki-dee given by the male as mating season approaches and from which it gets its common name. Grayish-brown above, the best identifying characteristic of this bird is the white breast with two black bands. Open fields, pastures, parking lots, or railroad grades provide nesting locations. The nest consists of a small hollow and usually contains three to five speckled eggs. If danger to the nest is imminent, the adult runs some distance away, spreads and depresses its tail, holds up one wing and drags itself along the ground while uttering a distress call. This display is intended to draw the intruder from the nest.

Semipalmated Plover 8"
Killdeer broken wing act

Killdeer 6"

American Golden Plover

Pluvialis dominica

This plover is seen only as a scarce transient about mid-May while on its spring migration between South America and the tundra of northwest North America. The fall migration takes them east to Nova Scotia and then south along the Atlantic coast to their wintering grounds in Argentina. In open meadows, small groups can be found feeding on insects or resting in the sun. When located, they are difficult to approach and will take flight for little reason. Another species, the black-bellied plover, is also found in the Northern Rockies and can be distinguished by its lighter, speckled-black back.

Marbled Godwit

Limosa fedoa

In its preference for alkaline prairie sloughs, the marbled godwit feeds along the shoreline of shallow water, probing for insects, worms, mollusks, or crustaceans. Its long, slightly upcurved bill allows for a deeper penetration of the muddy bottom than do the bills of most other shorebirds. Short dry-grass prairies are also areas for feeding on insects, and it is here, well back from water, that nesting takes place. In a shallow depression near a rock or clump of weeds, either sex will sit tight on the eggs. Their color pattern of brown weaved with black conceals them from potential predators. If discovered, they burst into the air with shrill alarming cries. Should harassment continue, they will turn and attack the trespasser's head.

Long-billed Curlew

Numenius americanus

With a curved bill some eight inches long, it seems it would have to be careful not to walk into anything, but the long-billed curlew displays amazing dexterity as it uses its bill to pluck insects from the short-grass plains. The shorelines of lakes, rivers, and ponds allow it to probe deep into mud for shellfish and worms, but the grasslands are its real home. Nests for the long-billed curlew are out in the open and well exposed. As the female incubates, she relies on her color for concealment, and can almost be touched before she will flutter off and do a broken-wing act. The hatched young are precocious and follow their parents just a few hours after emerging from the egg.

American Golden Plover 9"   T. ULRICH
Marbled Godwit 16"   T. ULRICH

Long-billed Curlew 19"   T. ULRICH

Willet   *Catoptrophorus semipalmatus*

A somewhat close cousin to the yellowlegs, willets will habituate the same wet meadows and prairie sloughs of lower valleys. Very conspicuous and noisy, these self-assertive birds have a large repertoire of distinctive calls. Even while standing or probing mud for worms, there are repetitive yipping noises. Any intruder sends them into the air where they emit a different scolding clamor which often warns other species. They like to fly in loose flocks, but once landed will scatter to feed alone. Nests are usually placed well back from water next to a rock or small bush. After hatching, young remain nearby as the adults forage for insects.

Greater Yellow-legs   *Tringa melanoleuca*

Often associating with other shorebirds along prairie sloughs or lakeshores, greater yellow-shanks are the sentinels, keeping a sharp lookout at all times. When an intruder is encountered, yellow-legs are the first to flush and spread alarm to other birds. Once considered a gamebird, their uneasiness had hunters labeling them "tattler" or "telltale." Most nesting is north of the United States border. Those seen in the Northern Rockies are usually traveling to and from their breeding grounds. Frequently observed feeding, they walk about and pick small fish from below the surface rather than probe the mud with their long bills. Their long legs and larger size distinguish them from the smaller mimic, lesser yellow-legs *(Tringa flavipes)*. Both are mirror images in appearance, habits, and flight and are easiest to identify when both species are together.

Willet 13½"
Willet flying

Greater Yellow-legs 11"

Least Sandpiper
Calidris minutilla

Snapping up insects or probing for larva in mud, the least sandpiper frequents the open sloughs and mud holes of the Northern Rockies during its fall and spring migrations. Its small size is not the best identifying characteristic, as this can be confused with the semipalmated sandpiper. Distinctively yellow feet with no webs will separate the shorelines of lakes, usually in company with other peeps. When approached, they will peep well ahead of the intruder and when pressured will take flight as a unit, only to alight further down the shore.

Upland Sandpiper
Bartramia longicauda

Initially, this bird was named "Bartramian sandpiper" after seventeenth-century American naturalist William Bartram. No great lover of water, its haunts are dry grassy fields, where it lives chiefly on insects. These large undisturbed stretches of grassland also serve as their nesting area. Because of this habitat preference, their name was changed to "upland plover." At one time they were as common as the meadowlark; they were hunted for food, but the plough is really what diminished this species. Recently, because of their structure and relationship to sandpipers, the colloquial name has been changed one more time to upland sandpiper.

Spotted Sandpiper
Actitis macularia

Preferring the banks of clear running streams and rivers, the spotted sandpiper is the most widely distributed and best-known sandpiper. It will run along the rocky shore picking up insects, crustaceans, or small mollusks, only to stop every few moments to "teeter" by flexing its legs. When spooked, the bird will take flight in a wide arc low over the water, quickly returning to shore. In some vegetation near water, females create a small depression to hold its eggs. The precocious young can swim and will keep up with the adults shortly after hatching.

Long-billed Dowitcher
Limnodromus scolopaceus

Probing the bottom with a deliberate vertical jab of its long bill, a dowitcher wades the shallow water of a marsh or slough. The tip of its bill is extremely sensitive and can be manipulated to grasp aquatic worms or mollusks buried in mud. Insect larva and diving beetles supplement their diet. These instinctively gregarious birds remain in tight flocks; occasionally, other shorebird species may be close by. When alarmed, the long-billed dowitchers rise together in flight and stay together as they alight further away. The bird is generally seen as a transient, coming through on its spring and fall migrations.

78

Least Sandpiper 5"   T. ULRICH
Spotted with young 6"   T. ULRICH

Upland Sandpiper 10"   M. BURCHAM
Long-billed Dowitcher 10"   T. ULRICH

Common Snipe
Capella gallinago

The snipe can probe deep into mud and use its long sensitive bill to detect the slightest movement of a worm or small mollusk. When frightened, this bird will remain motionless and rely on its protective coloration to blend with the surroundings. Only when in danger of being trampled will it flush in erratic flight, uttering sharp nasal notes of alarm. Another very distinguising sound is made when the male snipe performs his courtship flight. Flying about in wide arcs with rapid wing beats, he suddenly makes a sharp downward dive with tail spread. Rushing air through this spread tail produces the non-vocal sound which either establishes its territory or attracts and holds a receptive female. The female builds her nest in grass near a marsh, muskeg, or slough — habitats which also serve as their feeding grounds.

Wilson's Phalarope
Phalaropus tricolor

Unlike most birds, there is a noteworthy reversal exhibited by the phalaropes. In this case, the female is brightly colored and carries on the courting. The drab male is left with the chore of building the nest, incubating, and caring for the young. Occasionally, a female will help with incubation as the male feeds along muddy or grassy edges or prairie sloughs. Venturing out to somewhat deeper water, a phalarope rotates in circles. This stirs the bottom and brings insect larva to the surface where they collect toward the center of the "whirlpool."

Franklin's Gull
Larus pipixcan

Named after a nineteenth-century English explorer, Sir John Franklin, this is one of our more beneficial and best-known gulls. It sometimes travels as far as 30 miles between its roosting marsh and the pastures or fields under plow where the Franklin's will forage for wireworms, cutworms, and insect grubs or larva. Later in the season they frequent prairies and grass fields to feed on grasshoppers and locusts caught on the wing. Highly gregarious among themselves, these gulls nest in compact colonies of immense numbers. Interestingly, they are also very sociable to other species, especially on their nesting grounds. Black terns, coots, rails, grebes, and various ducks also nest in close proximity.

Common Snipe 9"
Male Wilson's Phalarope 7½"

T. ULRICH
T. ULRICH

Franklin's Gull 11"

J. WASSINK

California Gull *Larus californicus*

The California gull and ring-billed gull *(Larus delawarensis)* are often found nesting together in large colonies on small islands of inland lakes. They can be distinguished from each other in that the California gull has green legs and lacks the noticeable ring around its bill. Both gulls are omnivorous and feed together at city dumps, along lake shores, open fields, or behind a plow. Their diet includes such delicacies as refuse, dead fish, road kills, insects, and worms. Even ducklings hatched near nesting colonies of gulls are invariably picked off long before they reach water. Interestingly, flocks of these same gulls, in 1848, devoured an invasion of black crickets in northern Utah. These crickets would have destroyed the Mormons' crops had it not been for californicus. Today, Utah's state bird is the California gull.

Herring Gull *Larus argentatus*

The herring gull is a casual visitor to the Rocky Mountain region. The best location for viewing one is usually at a larger lake or reservoir where they patrol the shorelines looking for dead fish or other carrion. Primarily scavengers, these gulls will also feed on berries, insects, crustaceans, frogs, and sometimes will parasitize other bird nests. Their crude stick nests lined with garbage are generally found in colonies on the islands of these larger lakes.

California Gull with young 17"
Ring-billed Gull 16"

T. ULRICH
J. WASSINK

Herring Gull 20"

T. ULRICH

Forster's Tern
Sterna forsteri

Similar to the common tern in appearance and habits, the Forster's tern is often overlooked by the casual observer. With ranges overlapping and having comparable nesting sites, positive identification is difficult. The leading edge of a Forster's forked tail is white, while that of a common is much darker. Also, upper surfaces of the wing at the base of the primaries show a more even gray. Nesting is in loose colonies, with sites often consisting of a floating mass of vegetation. Occasionally, the nest might be placed on a muskrat hut or small island. Feeding is accomplished by patrolling as they watch for small fish near the surface. Quick plunges breaking the surface produce minnows caught in their bills. History tells us this tern is named after an eighteenth-century naturalist, Johann Reinhold Forster, who sailed around the world with Captain Cook.

Caspian Tern
Sterna caspia

Caspian tern is the largest of inland terns. It frequents large lakes adequately stocked with small fish. Patrolling back and forth over the water, its bright red bill is pointed downward when fishing. Having spied a fish near the surface, a caspian will hover a moment before setting its wings for a headfirst dive into the water. Standing on a sandbar or nesting island, its short legs give it a squat appearance.

Black Tern
Chlidonias niger

Here in the northwestern United States, the black tern is characterized as an "aquatic swallow." Central Europe has this same bird and there it is called the "black-veiled fairy" of the wetlands. Its black head diminishes to gray at the tail feathers. This and its ability to swoop gracefully back and forth snapping damsel flies from the air make it not unlike a swallow. However, it can also be observed hovering over prey, snatching insects from the surface, or diving headlong into water as it feeds. Nests can be a floating raft of reeds and grasses or a cup of reeds atop a muskrat hut.

Forster's Tern 14"
Caspian Tern 20"

Black Tern 9"

Rock Dove

Columba livia

Initially, the rock dove was introduced from Europe, but pigeon fanciers have produced an incredible number of variants. In color, they may be anything from pure white to mirror images of the blue-gray original species. Feral rock doves are now established in most settled areas. Their poorly-constructed nests of straw and twigs are usually located on ledges of public buildings. Large numbers of nesting pairs may pose serious problems as excrement or nest debris collects over the years.

Mourning Dove

Zenaida macroura

The name "mourning dove" comes from a melodramatic cooing of the male during springtime courtship. Within his established territory the male also engages in display volleys that involve towering flights ended by gliding downward on outspread wings in a graceful arc. After courting, a frail platform nest of twigs is made upon which the female lays two white eggs. If startled from its nest while incubating, the adult may knock out one or both of the eggs. With a high nest mortality, nesting may continue well into summer. Young are fed with "pigeon milk" secreted in the crop of either adult. The sexes are very similar in appearance — light gray above and pale buffy below. Both have long, tapered tails fringed with white. Iridescense on the neck and a blue-to-gray crown are more prominent on the male.

Rock Dove 11"
Mourning Dove 10½"

Mourning Dove squabs

Screech Owl   *Otus kennicottii*

Otus will leave its darkened sanctuary only after dusk, spending the daylight hours in a hole in a tree or among the rafters of an abandoned building. Hunting around farm buildings for the mice and voles these structures attract, this owl is rarely noticed as it usually returns to its hiding place before dawn. The screech owl exhibits two distinct phases of color; red and gray. Both phases can be found in the same nest and the percentage of each appears to be equal.

Great Horned Owl   *Bubo virginianus*

Often nicknamed "cat owl" because of the large ear tufts, catlike eyes, and shape of the head, great horned is our most easily recognized owl. With a range covering most of North America, it inhabits the heavy woodlands and at times scattered patches of trees. Nocturnal, the great horned will perch quietly to hear the forest sounds. A faint scurry of a mouse will send this owl on a silent, swooping flight. With a quick downward thrust of its talons, it snatches an unsuspecting prey from the forest litter. A ravenous feeder, this bird will prey upon almost any living creature, except the large animals. Daytimes are spent roosting in the shadows of a conifer, hidden from the eyes of magpies and jays which would continually harass the sleepy owl. Nesting can take place as early as January and often a female, covered with snow, can be found incubating.

Long-eared Owl   *Asio otus*

Perched near a pine trunk, the protective coloration of a long-eared closely resembles a branch stub or piece of weather-beaten bark. This camouflage allows it to have an exceptional degree of boldness. People often venture to within feet and yet these owls remain. Additional protection is provided by its habitat: thick, almost impenetrable tangles of dense evergreen. Here this owl will remodel an old crow, magpie, or hawk nest to raise its young. Incubation begins when the first egg is laid, resulting in nestlings of different sizes. The last owlets have a great disadvantage and rarely survive attacks of their larger, hungry nestmates. As with most owls, the long-ear is nocturnal as it hunts for small mammals. Often confused with a great horned owl, it lacks a white collar and has ear tufts projecting from atop the head.

Great Gray Owl   *Strix nebulosa*

With a length approaching 34 inches and wing span almost twice that, great gray is termed our largest owl. Actually, neither its weight nor body size equals that of snowy or great horned owls. The great gray's large head, long tail, and fluffy plumage make this northern inhabitant appear bigger than it really is. Perched on a branch part way up a tree, the great gray hunts nocturnally along the forest margins and fields bordering them for mice and voles. A year-round resident, even winter's snow has little effect on its hunting abilities. It is estimated that a great gray owl, 50 yards away, can locate the sound of a moving mouse under as much as 18 inches of snow.

Screech Owl 8" J. WASSINK
Long-eared Owl 13" L. KAISER

Great Horned Owl 20" D. ON
Great Gray Owl 22" J. WASSINK

Barred Owl
Strix varia

The barred owl is a bottomland bird named for its heavily barred upper-parts. A large facial disc is accented by two obsidian eyes. A strictly nocturnal hunter, this owl locates prey by sound rather than sight. Its ear openings are remarkably large and differ slightly in size and shape. This adaptation aids in accurate location of a sound source and can detect the slightest rustle of a small mammal in the grass. Although this owl may be looking in the direction of a sound, it is actually focusing its ears and not its eyes, as vision is of secondary importance. The barred owl's diet is largely made up of small mammals of the night, so this species is definitely beneficial.

Saw-whet Owl
Aegolius acadicus

The outstanding characteristic of this owl is its tameness. The saw-whet can be approached to fairly close range, sometimes only inches, and has actually been caught in the hands. Rather difficult to find, it prefers dark coniferous forests, usually roosting just a few feet from the ground. Daylight is spent quietly hidden in a tree, but come darkness it listens for the rustle of small nocturnal mammals. Dependent on woodpecker holes for nest sites, the bird will also take to nest boxes if set in a secluded location. While roosting, saw-whet will deliver a series of notes much like the filing of a saw, and this call is responsible for its common name.

Pygmy Owl
Glaucidium gnoma

Unlike most other owls, the pygmy is active during daylight hours and especially at twilight and daybreak. From an inconspicuous perch on an evergreen near a clearing, this owl will drop down on the unsuspecting rodent, lizard, snake, or insect. Birds also make up a substantial part of its diet and occasionally it will attack ones larger than itself. This trait often causes many small birds to harass the owl as it sits around its favorite haunt. The female incubates her small clutch of eggs in an old woodpecker hole or other natural cavity in a tree.

Barred Owl 17"
Saw-whet Owl 7"

T. ULRICH
GNP

Pygmy Owl 6"

P. MENARD

Burrowing Owl
Athene cunicularia

Standing on a dirt mound created by some energetic prairie dog, the aptly-named burrowing owl is owner of the subterranean dwelling below. Eight to ten feet from the entrance, a crude nest of grass and roots cradles a large clutch of eggs. After hatching, the young will venture out in early summer to join their parents on the mound. Any sign of danger sends them scurrying back into the burrow. Nearly all hunting is done either during first light or after dusk; the owl often perches on a fencepost listening for prey rustling in the grass below. Occasionally, the burrowing owl will hover in flight during hunting, in a manner similar to that of a kestrel or kingfisher.

Common Nighthawk
Chordeiles minor

A member of the goatsucker family, nighthawks have an extremely small bill with an enormous mouth. Gaining speed with a few quick wing beats, they dart through a cloud of flying insects. With mouths gaping from ear to ear, they hawk huge numbers of the flying arthropods. Active mostly at twilight and dawn, they can be easily identified by their notched tail and long pointed wings marked with a distinctive white wing bar. Mottled brown and black, this protective coloration is utilized when resting on the ground, nesting, or sitting lengthwise on a limb. Their common name is derived from the swift flight and long wings so similar to those of a hawk.

Burrowing Owl 8"
Common Nighthawk 9"

Nighthawk resting

Rufous Hummingbird   *Selasphorus rufus*

With its range extending as far north as Alaska, the rufous hummingbird
is the most common hummer found in the Northern Rockies. As a male
arrives here in early spring, his feeding and nesting territory is defended
with vigor, even against other species of birds. When an available female
enters his domain, a series of high diving and rising loops signal his
courtship. Swooping just inches from her, the suitor displays a brilliant
ruby red gorget. If accepted, a small cup-shaped nest of lichen stuck
together with spiderweb is constructed on a low evergreen bough. Two
eggs are laid with the female doing all rearing of the young. A true marvel
of nature when it comes to flying, a hummer's wings beat some eighty
times a second.

Male Rufous Hummer 3½"　　　　　　　　　T. ULRICH
Female Rufous Hummer　　　　　　　　　　T. ULRICH

Rufous Hummer at nest　　　　　　　　　　T. ULRICH

Calliope Hummingbird   *Stellula calliope*

Stellula, meaning "little star," developed from the trait of the male calliope to fan out its purple gorget feathers above its chest when excited. An
example is observed in the courting. Back and forth he swoops like a
pendulum exhibiting this visual display. He defends his territory very
courageously, but once the eggs are laid, he loses interest and departs for
other conquests. The small cup-shaped nest with one or two young is solely
tended by the female as she feeds them a fluid food from her crop. One
interesting fact is that the wings of this bird when flying beat about eighty
times a second. These wings oscillate so fast they appear as a blur and the
air they move becomes a hum to the ears.

Belted Kingfisher   *Megaceryle alcyon*

Sitting motionless on a perch with bill pointed downward, the kingfisher
watches for fish in waters below. Suddenly it drops and with a vibrant
splash hurtles into the water. Moments later it surfaces with a luckless
minnow in its bill. This persistent and skillful practice of catching fish has
made the kingfisher admired by most fishermen. A solitary bird by nature, the kingfisher knows every perch and branch where an immediate
view of its fishing grounds can be obtained. Fishing by sight, their waters
must be clear enough for prey to be seen. Easily identified by a bright
white collar, the kingfisher owes its Latin name alcyon to an old fable of
classical mythology. Alcyone, daughter of Aeolus, grieved so deeply when
her husband perished in a shipwreck that she threw herself into the sea,
and was immediately changed into a kingfisher.

Male Calliope Hummer 3"   T. ULRICH
Calliope Hummer at nest   T. ULRICH

Female Calliope Hummer   T. ULRICH
Belted Kingfisher 12"   GNP

Common Flicker

Colaptes auratus

Because of interbreeding where their ranges overlap, the red-shafted flicker and its eastern counterpart, the yellow-shafted, have been newly classified as the common flicker. Any difference in its habitat, nesting, or feeding habits is due to the difference in environment. Color pattern is similar for both species, but coloration is noticeably different. The underside of the wings and tail of the "yellowhammer" is a brilliant golden-yellow, combined with a red crescent on the nape, and black mustache on the male. The red-shafted is salmon red below its wings and tail, and the male has a red mustache. All hybrids will show a blended or mixed variety of patterns, and will be consistently asymmetrical with opposite sides of the bird being different. The favorite haunts of the flicker are open country or lightly wooded regions. It has taken well to human intrusion and can be found among farms, villages, small towns, or even in some of the smaller cities. Possible nesting cavity sites are unlimited, from dead snags, telephone poles and walls of buildings, to burrows in the bank of a creek. Feeding is more directed toward probing for ants and grubs, rather than actually drilling wood like most other woodpeckers do.

Pileated Woodpecker

Dryocopus pileatus

Pileatus means crested, a reference to the prominent tuft of red which extends back from the top of the head of a pileated woodpecker. This characteristic separates it from all other woodpeckers in the Northern Rockies. In flight, bright white lower wing patches are visible. The sexes can be distinguished by the male's red mustache, which extends from the base of his lower bill. The pileated's long slender neck enables it to hold its head farther back, allowing it to make powerful strokes with its heavy bill. A permanent resident, this bird prefers the same nesting location, even the same tree trunk, year after year. Because of this, cavities usually ascend the trunk with openings somewhat triangular in shape.

Male Red-shafted Flicker 10½" T. ULRICH
Male Yellow-shafted Flicker   T. ULRICH

Female Red-shafted Flicker   T. ULRICH
Pileated with young 15"   T. ULRICH

Downy Woodpecker   *Picoides pubescens*

One of our more common woodpeckers, a downy enjoys coniferous as well as deciduous forests for feeding and cavity nesting. This permanent resident is identified by its vivid black and white colors. A black forehead continuing over the top of its head and a black streak through the eye contrast with its white face. The downy's bill is shorter than its head and is used mainly for chiseling or prying bark away in search of insects. A similar species is the larger hairy woodpecker. With a bill as long as its head, a hairy is more of a driller. This major difference allows both to inhabit the same area and not compete with each other. Interestingly, the male of both species has a characteristic red nape.

Hairy Woodpecker   *Picoides villosus*

This bird is an enlarged model of the familiar downy woodpecker. The one major difference in separating them is that the hairy has a bill as long as its head, used primarily for drilling. Pure white outer tail feathers are a good diagnostic characteristic. Like the small downy, males have a distinct red notch at the back of the head. One unique characteristic of this bird has to do with its tongue. The tip is a rigid, barbed lance which can be thrust out a great distance. Upon drilling a hole, injection of the tongue will pierce a grub, quickly pulling it back into the bill.

White-headed Woodpecker   *Picoides albolarvatus*

Indigenous to the western United States, the white-headed woodpecker is an incidental along the western edge of our Northern Rockies, where it prefers the giant Ponderosa pine and Douglas fir. Examining crevices in the trees, picking ants from the surface of bark, and prying bark away for hidden insects are a few of its feeding techniques. In flight a large patch of white in the wing is conspicuous, but this shows as a narrow stripe on the wing when perched. The male is easily identified; any indication of red on its nape denotes its masculine gender.

Northern Three-toed Woodpecker *Picoides tridactylus*

There are two species of three-toed woodpeckers inhabiting the Northern Rockies. This woodpecker has white bars across its back which distinguish it from the solid black back of the black-backed three-toed woodpecker. In both species, the male has a golden crown. An Alaskan Indian legend tells of a male three-toed devouring his mate in a time of famine. He wiped his claws on the top of his head and today still carries a yellow "mark of the fat." Compared to other woodpeckers, the three-toed is very silent and usually passes by unnoticed. Infrequent use of its voice and its soft pecking blows, which do not carry far, soundwise, add to its low profile. A year-round resident, it is not afraid of cold weather or hard work — it often chisels into solid wood for the larva of wood boring beetles. Old burn areas are favorite haunts of this woodpecker. Here numerous snags provide many places for this bird to excavate a nest hole, occasionally only eight to ten feet above ground.

Downy Woodpecker 6"   T. ULRICH
White-headed Woodpecker 8"   T. ULRICH

Hairy Woodpecker 7½"   T. ULRICH
Northern Three-toed 7½"   D. ON

Lewis Woodpecker
Melanerpes lewis

Often confused with a crow, this woodpecker uses the same slow, even steady flight. It prefers open country with large trees such as Ponderosa pine. Unlike most woodpeckers, it chooses to perch atop fenceposts or stumps. Although it is fully equipped to peck at wood for food, the Lewis woodpecker is a master at catching insects on the wing. It will also feed on and store acorns. While most of the body is black (greenish in strong light), the best means for identifying this bird are the gray collar and the upper gray breast which descends into rose.

Yellow-bellied Sapsucker
Sphyrapicus varius

The yellow-bellied is most often recognized by the concentric holes drilled in live birch, aspen, and poplar. This sapsucker will repeatedly return to feed on sap flowing freely from wounds made on a tree or will eat the insects trapped by this sap. This bird is identified by a distinctive white wing bar, a mottled black-and-white back, a red forehead and throat, and a black chest explicitly separated from the yellowish belly. Only a summer resident here in the Northwest, many think this bird causes untold damage to trees by drilling the checkerboard holes. These holes do penetrate the bark, cambium, and sometimes the wood, but only rarely will a tree die. Aesthetic value is the main concern here, because the yellow-bellied sapsucker does scar the bark with pits.

Williamson's Sapsucker
Sphyrapicus thyroideus

In the early 1850s, two species of sapsucker were provided with distinctly different names. Some two decades later it was noticed both species were occupying the same tree cavity at the same time. One was definitely a Williamson's sapsucker. The brown-headed ladder-backed plumage of the other turned out to be "Mrs. Williamson." This resulted in the elimination of one unnecessary species. Williamson's will bore for sap as does its cousin, the yellow-bellied. But insects and succulent inner cambium are the chief components of is diet. Mated birds will return, year after year, to the same nesting site. As the female incubates, the male Williamson's sits nearby to warn her with a series of taps should danger arise. Males can also be differentiated from other four-toed woodpeckers by the lack of any red feathers in the head region.

Lewis Woodpecker 9"   T. ULRICH
Male Williamson's Sapsucker 8"   D. ON

Yellow-bellied Sapsucker 8"   T. ULRICH
Female Williamson's Sapsucker   D. ON

Eastern Kingbird

Tyrannus tyrannus

With a scientific label like tyrannus, the kingbird's vicious aggressiveness toward any bird that flies into its territory is well-recognized. Even if much larger in size, the intruder is met with savage, swooping assaults and harsh, screaming cries. Other birds will defend for the same reason, but none are as fearless and persistent as the kingbird. This bird frequents lightly wooded areas interspersed with open fields and meadows. Here it can be easily identified by a black tail tipped with white. Perched in the open on a wire, fencepost, or dead limb, a kingbird has an unobstructed view of the surrounding area. Dashing out to catch a passing insect, it will likely return to the same vantage point. A large portion of its diet consists of harmful insects.

Hammond's Flycatcher

Empidonax hammondii

Experience, sharp eyes, and the faculty to notice slight differences in color and body contours will help in distinguishing the many different flycatchers. For the novice, nesting season is the best time to field-identify many of these species. The Hammond's is fond of mature coniferous forests at high elevations. Its nest, made of plant fibers lined with grass, is usually more than 25 feet from the ground. Much of this flycatcher's time is spent active amidst upper branches, but it will also perch in the open, where it will fly out and capture insects on the wing. A very similar species, the dusty flycatcher, prefers the foothills and is most commonly found in alder and willow thickets, but even this criteria is not infallible.

Horned Lark

Eremophila alpestris

For this lark, the "horns" which at times may be hard to see, are actually short feather tufts behind each ear. During courtship, these tufts are fully erect. A strutting show, aerial display, and non-musical singing are more techniques used to allure receptive females during breeding season. Short-grass prairies is the preferred habitat where the lark can walk freely, stopping often to investigate its surroundings while feeding on weed seed and insects.

Eastern Kingbird 7"
Hammond's Flycatcher 4½"

Horned Lark 6½"

Barn Swallow   *Hirundo rustica*

Originally the barn swallow nested in caves and on rocky faces of cliffs. With the coming of man, it has abandoned these primitive sites and now utilizes the shelter of buildings and bridges. On a rafter or against a wall, this swallow plasters its nest. Small pellets of mud from the edge of farm ponds or barnyard puddles are reinforced with straw and built up layer upon layer. Shaping the cup with its body, the barn swallow lines the nest with fine grasses and feathers. The site must be sheltered from rain because any wetness would cause it to disintegrate. The barn swallow is easly identified by its long outer tail feathers as it hawks both low and high for flying insects. After nesting, this bird gathers in flocks with other swallows, frequenting marshes and shallow sloughs in preparation for a fall migration to South America.

Violet-green Swallow   *Tachycineta thalassina*

Closely resembling a tree swallow, the very abundant violet-green has developed an attraction toward human settlement. Readily taking to nest boxes or various locations around buildings, it tolerates close proximity to its own kind as well as other swallows. Several species can be seen performing swooping twists and turns over a nearby lake hawking for insects. In flight, violet-green swallows are easily identified from all the others by a white-sided rump. Very susceptible to cold weather, most of these swallows have left for Central America by late August.

Barn Swallow 6"
Violet-green Swallow 5"

Cliff Swallow collecting mud

Cliff Swallow
Hirundo pyrrhonota

Master masons when it comes to constructing their nests, cliff swallows are a most industrious species. Numbers of them will hover over the edge of a puddle, scooping mud with their mouths. This mud will be formed into pellets and plastered against a cliff overhang, barn, eave of a house, or underside of a bridge. Occasionally, sandy soil will hinder construction of these nests as the structures soon crumble, sometimes losing a whole clutch. These somewhat bottle-shaped adobes are often clustered into groups — often as many as several hundred. With the advance of cooler weather which decreases insect populations, cliff swallows and their allies migrate south to spend the winter deep in South America.

Bank Swallow
Riparia riparia

Most swallows will take to man-made structures, but the closest to anything man-influenced that a bank swallow will approach are road or railway cuts. Just as with a natural precipice, these man-made cliffs become home for hundreds of gregarious bank swallows. The burrows, slightly elevated at the end for a nesting chamber, are often less than a foot apart and can measure up to four feet deep. Swooping and gliding over the cliffs, hawking for insects, both parents' efforts are needed to satisfy the nearly insatiable appetites of their young.

Tree Swallow
Tachycineta bicolor

One of the first swallows to arrive in spring, the tree swallow will also stay longer before fall migration than its close cousins. Earliest to arrive are males, followed a few weeks later by females. After some pursuit of the females above treetops, males try to entice any receptive one to inspect a tree cavity as a potential nest site. Incubation is controlled by the females while the opposite sex perch alone nearby. Insects comprise most of the swallow's diet and are largely caught on the wing. Small beaks conceal gaping mouths excellent for scooping tiny-winged invertebrates. Frequently, tree swallows feed over water for an almost-constant emergence of insects. With the destruction of natural habitat by lumbering and agriculture, tree swallows have adapted to nest boxes, but this puts them in competition with house sparrows and starlings.

Gray Jay
Perisoreus canadensis

The names gray jay, Canada jay, whiskey jack, or camp robber all refer to a friendly rogue that will visit your campsite. Enjoyable and amazing at first, this can change to torment as they ravage food from the table or even frying bacon from a pan. They appear silently from nowhere and watch fearless as a meal is prepared. Any pilfered food not eaten immediately is carried away and cached in some secret hollow or as a "bolus" stuck among the needles of an evergreen. Small family units of fledglings and adults will appear with the onset of spring because nesting is early. In March, with snow on the ground and sub-freezing temperatures, females incubate on well-feathered, insulated nests.

Cliff Swallow 5" J. WASSINK
Tree Swallow 5" T. ULRICH

Bank Swallow 5" J. WASSINK
Gray Jay 10" T. ULRICH

Pinyon Jay
Gymnorhinus cyanocephalus

The pinyon jay is only seen as a casual visitor to the Northern Rocky Mountains. Because its shape, walk, and flight resemble those of a crow so closely, it is often nicknamed "blue crow." Except when nesting, this jay travels in flocks searching for seeds in pines, berries in season, or insects. When natural foods are scarce, the pinyon may flock to cultivated fields and do considerable damage to grain crops. Interestingly, at one time this bird was known as Maximilian's jay when discovered in Montana about 1833 by German naturalist, Maximilian.

Steller's Jay
Cyanocitta stelleri

The steller is found in coniferous forests at altitudes of 4,000 feet or more. This bird retains the bold, greedy, and domineering qualities similar to those of its eastern cousin, the blue jay. Especially during breeding season it becomes a destructive poacher, seeking out and cannibalizing the eggs and young of smaller birds. In winter its habits change. Competition is stiff. Any food small in size is swallowed whole, while larger pieces are hammered into more manageable fragments. Feeding stations are frequented, and although they become accustomed to human presence, they still retain a natural wariness.

Clark's Nutcracker
Nucifraga columbiana

Back in 1805, the Lewis and Clark Expedition described Clark's nutcracker as a "new species of woodpecker." Later in the same century it carried the name "Clark's crow." Both these names were appropriate and refer to a crow-like behavior and ability to cling like a woodpecker while looking for grubs or hammering open a cone. Regular residents of the pinyon-juniper zone, they prefer high mountain country up to 13,000 feet. Nutcrackers fly in loose groups except during nesting season. When not feeding on insects, seeds, berries, carrion, or even small mammals, their omnivorous feeding habits draw them to campgrounds and visitor centers where they compete for food scraps with Canada jays.

Pinyon Jay 9"
Steller's Jay 11"

T. ULRICH
D. ON

Clark's Nutcracker 10"

T. ULRICH

Black-billed Magpie
Pica pica

Although despised for its disagreeable traits as thief and scavenger, the magpie is also admired for its attractiveness. This bird has remained one of the best known species. A large portion of its diet is carrion, but it also takes a heavy toll on agricultural pests such as cutworms, wireworms, and grasshoppers. Still, its bad reputation hangs on, and organized campaigns try, with little effect, to decrease the population. Such attempts have made the magpie justifiably wary of man; it is almost impossible to approach. The scientific name pica, meaning black and white, suits the bird well. A black body (iridescent in strong light) contrasts with the white lower breast, white sides, and scapulars. In flight, its long tail extends straight out behind, but is elevated when the bird walks on the ground.

Common Raven
Corvus corax

Ravens can be found throughout the Northern Rockies during all times of the year. During nesting season they retreat to more remote locations where they become rather inconspicuous, but anyone in the back country has a good chance of seeing one. Opportunistic feeders, they eat just about anything, from seeds, berries and insects, to refuse. They also patrol highways for road kills or wilderness areas for winter-killed carrion. Ravens are exceptional at aerial gymnastics with much time spent riding the thermals like an eagle. Their nesting habits are also similar to raptors. A raven nest is usually located on the face of a cliff and is rather bulky, made of sticks lined with any soft material. A crow may be confused with this species, because it is similar in appearance, but crows are 25 percent smaller than ravens and have a different call.

Black-billed Magpie 18"
Common Raven 21"

Ravens feeding on lichen

Black-capped Chickadee   *Parus atricapillus*

A permanent year-round resident, the best time for viewing black-capped is during winter, when they frequent feeding stations. Yielding to most other birds without an argument, they will return promptly when the way is clear. Anything not eaten immediately is carried away and stored behind cracks in bark or among curled dry leaves. Their natural winter diet is found examining bark or branches for spider eggs, cocoons, or dormant insects. During summer, chickadees feed mainly on insects, seeds, and wild berries. They prefer to excavate their own cavity in a dead tree stump for a nest site.

Mountain Chickadee   *Parus gambeli*

Winter brings an overlap to the ranges of mountain and black-capped chickadees. The mountain chickadee can be differentiated from its counterpart by a distinctive narrow white line above its eye. During nesting season, these little birds choose open coniferous woods at high elevations. Cavities in trees or old woodpecker holes conceal the nest lined with moss and fur. They are easily overlooked because short fluttering flights from tree to tree make up most of the bird's activity.

Ruby-crowned Kinglet   *Regulus calendula*

One of the best identifying characteristics of this bird is the bright ruby crown of the male, but the difficulty is that this crown is only visible when he is excited or during courtship. Watch for any kind of yellow on the top of its head since this would designate a close relative, the golden-crowned kinglet. Next, look for a bright white eye ring which is usually broken at the top. This is a distinguishable trait readily noticeable on a ruby-crowned. These birds are very prolific and most of the warmer season will find them in any type of woods. Come breeding season, they prefer coniferous forests as both sexes hang a mossy cup-like nest among the smaller twigs. Clutches are usually large, numbering seven to nine, and after hatching it takes all the energy of both parents to feed their hatchlings. Continually in search of insects, they habitually flick their wings in a nervous manner.

Black-capped Chickadee 4½"
Mountain Chickadee 4"

Ruby-crowned Kinglet 3½"

Dipper (Water Ouzel)   *Cinclus mexicanus*

The dipper is amazing to everyone. Without the aid of webbed feet or any
of the other special adaptations of water birds, the dipper is as much at
home under water as other birds are in the air. Insulated with a soft, thick
plumage and an enlarged preen gland to keep the feathers well oiled, even
winter's cold has little effect. The dipper is a solitary bird and always lives
near falling, cascading, or rapid, clear-running streams, but sometimes a
quiet pool is home. It can use its short wings to swim underwater to catch
insect larva or an occasional minnow. The dipper also possesses the ability
to walk underwater. One theory believes the actual current pushing on its
back holds it down. Coming to the surface it swims for a dry place to climb
out. From its characteristic bobbing motion evolved the common name
"dipper." When disturbed, it flies low over the water, winding with the
stream.

Dipper (Water Ouzel) 6"   T. ULRICH
Dipper (Water Ouzel)   T. ULRICH

Dipper nestlings   T. ULRICH

White-breasted Nuthatch
Sitta carolinensis

Largest and most widely distributed of North America's five nuthatches is the white-breasted. Year round this bird searches the trunks and limbs of deciduous trees for hidden larva and insect eggs. Moving upward, downward, or sideways with great agility, it creeps about on the rough bark exploring every crevice with its long, pointed, slender bill. Its ability to assume the inverted position is due to the soft flexibility of its tail feathers in not being able to use them as a prop. Woodpeckers have stiff tail feathers and use them as a brace to support the upright position. It also enables the woodpecker to impact a stronger blow with its bill than can be delivered by the nuthatch. Thus, most of what this little tree mouse eats is superficial. A permanent resident, the nuthatch will nest in a natural cavity or one it can excavate.

Red-breasted Nuthatch
Sitta canadensis

Sometimes called the "upside down bird," this little creature most often climbs down the trunk and peers at its world with body pointing downward and head slightly uplifted. Much of its life is spent in the upper canopies of the coniferous forest. Here it creeps among the branches and upper trunk investigating bark fissures for insects, which comprise most of its diet. Frequently accompanied by chickadees in its search for food, nuts and sunflower seeds will lure the bird to a feeding station. Due to small size, it has to chisel a cavity nest, usually plastering the opening with fir resin or pitch. Winter changes the underparts to a rich rusty brown, but this will fade as spring encroaches. A black eye bar will distinguish it from all other nuthatches.

Pygmy Nuthatch
Sitta pygmaea

These little gray nuthatch midgets keep mostly to the Ponderosa pine forest of the West. In a typical upside-down nuthatch position, they probe and pry for hidden insects from trunks. Picking off insects on the wing or those sitting on twigs will also supplement their diet. With such close activity on pine-resined surfaces, these pygmies usually have pitch-stained yellow breasts. They use a small cavity in a dead stump for a nest, and upon fledging will gather in small flocks to roam the forests with chickadees, warblers, and creepers.

Brown Creeper
Certhia americana

Its small size, neutral plumage, soft voice, and routine creeping habits combine to make the brown creeper one of the unobtrusive inhabitants of the deep woods. Creeping a spiral course up a tree trunk, they investigate for the insects and insect eggs hidden in the bark of conifers. Their weak beak is used as tweezers to pluck these insects, which could threaten the life of the tree. A creeper will wedge a small twig nest under a loose flake of bark to hold its eggs.

White-breasted Nuthatch 5"   T. ULRICH
Pigmy Nuthatch 3½"   T. ULRICH

Red-breasted Nuthatch 4"   T. ULRICH
Prown Creeper 5"   A. NELSON

House Wren
Troglodytes aedon

Early settlers that first experienced this noisy bundle of energy were reminded of one they knew in England. Named after the Old World relative, "Jenny" is a common name that is still heard today. So well does this little bird take to human intrusion, that small birdhouses set up near some shrubbery are soon occupied. The male initiates nest building. But a shrewd female often "argues" and changes the structure to suit her own taste. Often disheartened, the male fills other local nest boxes. Then he uses the nests to either take up with another female or to discourage other birds from nesting too close to the original one. In the wild, house wrens use natural tree cavities or old woodpecker holes. They feed almost exclusively on insects, many of which are harmful.

Long-billed Marsh Wren
Cistofhorus palustris

As with all wrens, the long-billed marsh wren is a compulsive songster and is usually heard long before it can be seen. Spending much of its life fluttering about the tangled marsh vegetation a few inches above water, it finds an abundance of insects and larva. These reedy confines also provide the female with an appropriate area to build her unique nest. The structure, large and globular, is constructed of woven reeds or cattails. Open on one side, it serves to support her clutch. When you approach, there is a chance to catch sight of this nervous little bird as it ascends a stem to inspect the intruder. Quickly it drops back down into the reedy confines while giving a scolding clatter.

Swainson's Thrush
Catharus ustulatus

The best recognizable field marks for a Swainson's thrush are buffy eye rings, cheeks, and breast. A similar close relative that can be found in the same mountain woodland area is a hermit thrush, identified by a paler eye ring with more overall olive-brown coloration. Much of their time is spent on the ground, running over the damp, shaded coniferous floor in search of ants, beetles, crickets, or other ground insects. A bulky nest of grass, leaves, and moss is constructed, usually not over seven feet from the ground.

House Wren 4"
Long-billed Marsh Wren 4"

Swainson's Thrush 6"

Mountain Bluebird   *Sialia currucoides*

When a male mountain bluebird flies from a fence post and splashes the countryside with sky blue, the beauty of his color brings an exclamation of delight from a casual observer. A white belly and black bill and feet vary from his turquoise plumage. The only blue a female exhibits is on her wings, tail, and rump with the rest of her body somewhat dullish toward brown. She prefers a cavity nest most often using an old woodpecker hole. Feeding is accomplished by sitting on conspicuous perches in open meadows, where they can drop down for insects. One other species this bird may be confused with is the western bluebird. Any chestnut brown on the breast will distinguish it as the latter.

Western Bluebird   *Sialia mexicana*

This bluebird has a much deeper blue than its close relative the mountain bluebird. Its rich chestnut brown on the breast circling around the upper back is an ideal characteristic in separating the two. Frequenting open woodlands, all nesting is in natural cavities or old woodpecker holes. This is one bird easily attracted to nest boxes and will defend vigorously against any other species which may try to take it over. Western bluebird likes to perch on a limb or fence post commanding a wide view of the surrounding area. Repeatedly it darts out to capture a passing insect and immediately returns to its lookout.

American Robin   *Turdus migratorius*

With an unlimited distribution, conspicuous orange-red breast, a reputation as a habinger of spring, and a tolerance for human inteference, the robin is certainly our best known American bird. Most often viewed on lawns picking up an earthworm, it must also be realized a robin is a bird of the wilderness. It can be seen in many woodlands, but prefers a forest edge, especially near water. A redbreast diet is split between animal matter and small fruits, with a favorite taste for earthworms. In a stick nest, molded with mud on the inside by rotations of the female, speckle-breasted nestlings are fed constantly. Due to this spotting in the young, classification relates the robin to thrushes. A further relation is revealed by its Latin name, meaning "migratory thrush."

Male Mountain Bluebird 6"   T. ULRICH   **Female Mountain Bluebird**   T. ULRICH
Male Western Bluebird 5½"   J. WASSINK   **Robin 8"**   T. ULRICH

Cedar Waxwing   *Bombycilla cedrorum*

Waiting for the wild berry crop to ripen, the cedar waxwing is usually later than most birds in nesting. A large part of the diet fed to nestlings consists of succulent small fruits, supplemented with insects. Nesting has been documented as late as mid-August. Most of the year these birds are seen in flocks of 40 or more, turning and twisting in flight only to alight in a treetop or on a telephone wire, all facing the same way. A popular activity often seen is the passing of a ripe berry from one to another all along the line and then back again. This passing of fruit seems to be a leisure event or possibly an extension of the berry-passing used in courtship. The cedar waxwing can be identified by its long brown crest either elevated or depressed, black mask and chin, yellowish belly, and a distinct yellow terminal tail band. The Bohemian waxwing is somewhat larger, more gray below, and is primarily a winter resident.

Cedar Waxwing 6"
Bohemian Waxwing 5½"

T. ULRICH
J. WASSINK

Waxwings"

T. ULRICH

Loggerhead Shrike
Lanius ludovicianus

With a beak hooked like an eagle's, the loggerhead is one of the most vicious birds for its size. A definite predator, it prefers to feed on small rodents, snakes, insects, and even other birds. One unique characteristic of this bird is its weak feet. Because it cannot hold prey, its victim must be impaled on a thorn or barbed wire so it can be pulled to pieces. Somewhat two-toned with white below and gray above, it is best identified by a wide black face mask. A summer resident here, it should not be confused with a larger species, the northern shrike. The northern species tends to be more of a winter resident, spending the summer nesting in northern Canada.

Loggerhead Shrike on nest 7"
Loggerhead Shrike hooking mouse

Loggerhead Shrike impaling mouse

Yellow-rumped (Audubon's) Warbler

Dendroica coronata

A coniferous forest warbler, Audubon's is one of the earliest warblers to arrive in spring. Small flocks of colorful males, starting to acquire their breeding plumage, are the first to arrive. Eventually, a male will leave the group only to perch atop an evergreen and repeat his courtship song, claiming the surrounding territory as his own. A few days later a passing female is sure to be charmed by his somewhat monotonous effort. In a well-concealed spot she constructs a small nest of moss and grass. Their diet, which is the same as that fed to the nestlings, consists of a variety of insects caught in the air both high and low among the pines.

Yellow Warbler

Dendroica petechia

The yellow warbler is one of the few birds that resists the parasitic practice of a cowbird (see brown-headed cowbird). Most species make no effort to get rid of the egg and even feed the young cowbird as they would feed their own. This warbler has the practice of building a flooring over its eggs including any a cowbird will have deposited. These floorings can be built as many as three to five times in trying to defeat the cowbird. But in addition this, the yellow warbler has other reasons to win our affection and respect. Its rich yellow plumage, cheery song, and consumption of large quantities of caterpillars, beetles, and small worms often label it "wild canary." It takes to both town and country alike if water is near. Additionally, it needs prominent song perches, good feeding areas, and some dense shrubbery for escape cover. As soon as young have fledged, the fall migration takes them south, so by the first of August, all are gone.

Male Yellow-rumped Warbler 4½"   T. ULRICH
Female Yellow-rumped Warbler   T. ULRICH

Yellow Warbler 4"   T. ULRICH

Western Meadowlark

Sturnella neglect

There are possibly a dozen birds whose removal from the landscape woul
be noticed even by the casual observer, one of these being the meadowlar
This is especially true when its rich, loud melody signifies the arrival o
spring. Found in open country of the short grass prairies, its pure, clea
song can be heard for nearly half a mile. Then look for the bright yellow
breast with black, v-shaped neck band which easily identifies this com
mon bird. When approached on land they walk away intermittently flick
ing open the tail to show their white outer feathers. A sharp alarm note i
also uttered until it is forced to fly. The arched-over nest is expertl
concealed in dense grass.

Yellow-headed Blackbird

Xanthocephalus xanthocephalu

The song of the yellow-headeds is a totally remarkable, unmusical, an
almost un-bird-like effort. Perched on some swaying reeds in their terri
ory, they appear to be straining every nerve in an attempt to produce wha
appears to be a painful, drawn-out cry. So gregarious are their instinct
and so restrictive are their nesting requirements, that marshland ma
contain dozens of pairs fluttering about, but only a mile away not one ca
be seen. Females utilize reeds or rushes at lower levels of the marsh t
support the woven, bulky nests. Both adults feed the young a hearty diet o
insects obtained from the marsh or adjacent fields. Compared to th
brilliant male, the dimorphic female is a sooty brown above, while belo
she is streaked with a blend of white and yellow.

Red-wing Blackbird

Agelaius phoeniceu

The most casual observer recognizes this avian as a blackbird with red o
its wings. Early springtime finds prairie sloughs or cattail stands o
shallow lakes filled with the conspicuous and displaying red-wing male
Perched atop swaying reeds, males, with tails spread and half-opene
wings, show the brilliant red of their shoulders and sing their harsh ye
musical songs. Below, the brown females twitter about incubating o
weaving nests from dried vegetation. Territories are defended constantl
from other red-wings with frequent quarrels, but should a raven or haw
fly nearby, the red-wings unite to drive away that larger intruder. As lat
summer approaches, red-wings gather, usually with other species o
blackbirds, and descend on grain fields. Insects are also taken as flock
migrate southward menacing the ripened crops.

Common Starling

Sturnus vulgar

An estimated 100 starlings were released in New York City about 189
Forty years later they reached the eastern slopes of the Northern Rockie
and within ten years they were breeding throughout the mountain
Obviously competitive, the starling has taken a toll on such native specie
as bluebirds, woodpeckers, swallows, martins, and many others. Its earl
spring arrival and pugnacious attitude conquer the choice nesting hole
Equipped with a long and heavy tapered bill, backed by a strong head,
guards its territory jealously. When not nesting, large flocks will devou
commercial fruit such as cherries or grapes during their nomadic foray
but they can also be beneficial by taking destructive snails and man
different harmful insects.

Western Meadowlark 8½"   T. ULRICH
Red-wing Blackbird 7"   J. WASSINK

Yellow-headed Blackbird 8½"   T. ULRICH
Common Starling 6"   T. ULRICH

Brewer's Blackbird   *Euphagus cyanocephalus*

Natural habitat for the brewer's blackbird is prairies and open meadows or pastures, where scattered shrubbery or thickets provide good nest sites. It has adapted very well to human alterations of the environment, and is quite often seen foraging across lawns, golf courses, and city parks. Any land conveyed from bush or forest to plowing will be frequented in the search for grubs or insects. These birds will flip over stones to find insects beneath. There is some dismay that brewer's do noticeable damage to commercial fruit, such as cherries. As to the amount of fruit eaten, it should be considered fair return for the harmful insects or weed seeds also ingested.

Common Grackle   *Quiscalus quiscula*

When alone, the grackle is rather timid, but in small to large flocks a different image is created. They become cocky, bold, and ready as a group to harass anything smaller in size. Springtime finds them robbing the nests of other birds for eggs and nestlings. Just about anything else that can be devoured is food for the grackle, but when something to eat is scarce, not even smaller adult birds are safe. Nesting is in loose small colonies consisting of bulky nests woven with dried grasses and weed stems. After fledging, adults and young flock to go ravaging as they migrate south to their winter range. Often confused with a brewer's blackbird, this species has a much longer, heavy bill, bright yellow eyes, and when walking will hold its tail well off the ground.

Female Brewer's Blackbird 8"
Male Brewer's Blackbird

T. ULRICH
T. ULRICH

Common Grackle 11"

M. BURCHAM

Brown-headed Cowbird   *Molothrus ater*

The brown-headed cowbird has an unusual habit of parasitizing other bird nests. Lurking in the area of another's nest, a cowbird female will slip in when the owner leaves, lay an egg, and take off. The host species will react by covering the egg with new nest lining, totally deserting the nest, or most often will continue to incubate and hatch out a monster. Incubation is short at 12 or 13 days so the larger young brown-headed crowds out the host offspring or eggs. A voracious appetite keeps the foster parents ceaselessly working until the cowbird fledges and returns to its own kind. As their common name implies, this bird will associate with cattle. Either sitting on the backs of cows or horses, or walking nearby, it will capture insects attracted to livestock.

Western Tanager   *Piranga ludoviciana*

Nature has indeed been generous when it comes to the brilliant plumage of the male western tanager. His crimson head, yellow body, and black wings and tail rival the coloration of any tropical species. Except for occasional ventures to pluck berries or snatch an insect, this bird prefers to remain high in the sheltering canopy of tall coniferous forests. It is not a very active bird and when feeding will usually sit on a branch, moving only its head to look for insects among the foliage. Seeing one, it darts to that location and remains there until it sees another. These sedentary habits create an impression of a shy and secretive bird, but once seen it is not all that difficult to follow. It also nests in this high canopy, usually well out on a limb. A braided nest of twigs and pine needles, lined with grass, holds the incubating olive-green female. Interestingly, there seems to be a mixup in name with ludoviciana meaning Louisiana. No part of the tanagers range comes near this state; this refers back to when the Louisiana Territory stretched northward into what is now British Columbia.

Male Cowbird 6½" T. ULRICH
Male Western Tanager 6" T. ULRICH

Female Western Tanager T. ULRICH

Evening Grosbeak   *Hesperiphona vespertina*

An early observer once believed the evening grosbeak roosted during
daylight in the dark refuges of foliage and left them at the approach of
night. From this it received its pleasing, but totally misleading common
name. Equipped with a strong, heavy bill, the grosbeak has no trouble
crushing the hard shells of maple, elm, or dogwood to expose the soft seed
within. This bird is easily attracted to feeding stations by sunflower seeds
and is constantly bickering for position. Between feedings, the grosbeak
spends its time sitting about in trees, chirping constantly. The male is
easily distinguished from the female by a yellow band across his forehead
above the eyes.

Lazuli Bunting   *Passerina amoena*

A western relative to the indigo bunting, lazuli can be found anywhere
thickets of willow or dense undergrowths of chokecherry and rosebush
form breeding territories. Atop these impenetrable coverts the brilliant
male of blue, cinnamon, and white poses to sing his song. Below, in a nest
seldom more than a few feet from the ground, an inconspicuous female
incubates. She rarely ventures out into the open, but feeds in the shrubbery and on the ground. Summer diet is composed largely of larval and
adult insects supplemented with some small seeds. In winter the lazuli
migrates far south to Mexico.

Male Evening Grosbeak 7"   T. ULRICH
Female Evening Grosbeak   T. ULRICH

Male Lazuli Bunting 4½"   T. ULRICH

Cassin's Finch   *Carpodacus cassinii*

The haunts of the Cassin's finch are associated with the yellow-pine forest of higher montain regions. Due to being very similar to a close relative, the purple finch, in appearance, habitat, and behavior, they should both be closely observed. The Cassin's male is less reddish above and has an easily distinguishable two-note call which is unlike the single metalic note of the purple finch *(Carpodacus purpureus)*. Most activity is carried on either at low levels or at the tree tops. Nesting is conducted in large conifers and generally at the terminal end of a branch. *Carpodacus* comes from Greek and means "fruit biting"; appropriately, their diet is comprised of buds, berries, and seeds. Another interesting behavior is that they are often found associating with crossbills. In this area lives another close relative, the house finch *(Carpodacus mexicanus)*. This finch tends to take to urban areas and can damage fruit growing areas by indscriminately pecking ripened pears, cherries, apples, and peaches.

Male Cassin's Finch 6"   T. ULRICH
Male Purple Finch 5½"   T. ULRICH

Female Cassin's Finch   T. ULRICH
House Finch 5"   T. ULRICH

Pine Grosbeak   *Pinicola enucleator*

As the name pine grosbeak implies, this bird has a year-round preference for mountain coniferous forests. Migratory, they are seen in the Northern Rockies only as winter residents. Flying in small groups of ten or so, they use clear whistled calls to keep the flock together as they wander in their search for groves of pine or spruce. Extracting seeds from the cones, these grosbeaks will also remove seeds from berries or from crabapples of ornamental trees. A feeding station with sunflower seeds is an effective means for bird watchers to attract them for a closer look. Brilliant rosy-red males are noticeably dimorphic from the drab yellow-olive females.

Gray-crowned Rosy Finch   *Leucosticte tephrocotis*

If you wish to view this species in summer, venture well above timberline — you will find rosy finches at the edge of retreating snow, foraging for insects and seeds. A high altitude nester, any jumble of jagged boulders or a cliff face will do to conceal their nests of grasses, moss, and feathers. Early snows will gather the rosys into flocks and send them retreating to lower elevations. They feed mostly on the ground — when there is a blanket of snow, they utilize tall weeds or grain protruding above the surface.

Male Pine Grosbeak 7½"
Female Pine Grosbeak

T. ULRICH
T. ULRICH

Gray-crowned Rosy Finch 6"

A. NELSON

American Redstart

Setophaga ruticilla

The American redstart is a common warbler of the deciduous woodlands where it frequents dense underbrush usually near water. They are constantly in motion, fluttering after insects and picking caterpillars from leaves. Alighting, a male will spread his tail and half open his wings to show off his brilliant markings. Mrs. Redstart builds a nest of grass and shredded bark lined with plant fibers. In this, she will incubate her clutch of eggs.

Pine Siskin

Carduelis pinus

This small dark finch often goes unnoticed as it feeds quietly in weeds or the crowns of tall conifers throughout North America. The brown streaked plumage of the pine siskin is drab except for some yellow wing patches visible when in flight. These finches are very sociable and are usually found in small flocks. Even when nesting, several pairs will form a loose colony. The pine siskin is especially fond of dandelion and thistle seeds, also cherishing the seeds of pine, spruce, aspen, and poplar. Very nomadic in their wanderings, some years an evergreen mountain forest might be teeming with siskins, while the next year not one can be found in the whole district.

American Goldfinch

Carduelis tristis

Often called the "wild canary," an American goldfinch male is such a bright yellow and black that the most casual observer will become enthused. As it flashes across a field, alighting on a thistle, several more soon appear. They fill their crops with seeds of surrounding plants such as dandelions, bachelor buttons, and primrose, but their favorite is thistle. The production of these seeds generally triggers the rather late nesting season. Nestlings are fed almost entirely on seeds. Adults shuck the hard shells and swallow the seeds, later regurgitating a predigested "cereal" into the offsprings' throats. This late nesting allows for only one clutch a year. As fall approaches, these thistlebirds gather in flocks and drift southward. Feeding stations with thistle seeds attract and often keep these beautiful birds in areas for extended periods.

Male Redstart 4½"
Pine Siskin 4"

Male Goldfinch 4"

Red Crossbill

Loxia curvirostra

The common name, crossbill, refers to the crossed tips of the mandibles used primaily to pry out seeds from unopened cones. Red crossbills are regular inhabitants of deep coniferous forests, but are somewhat nomadic in their search for feeding areas. An invasion of crossbills into an area is determined largely by the cone crop. Very gregarious, they will move in and nest at any time of year. When cones are scarce, crossbills gather in flocks, wandering far south, feeding on garden evergreens along the way. It is legend that while Jesus was suffering crucification, a small bird alighted upon the cross and attempted to pull the nails from his hands and feet. The bird tried so hard its bill became badly twisted and its plumage covered with blood. That bird was the red crossbill.

Green-tailed Towhee

Pipilo chlorurus

Occasionally seen as an incidental, most observers pass this towhee off as an unidentified green-tailed sparrow because of its small size. Since first described as a finch by Audubon in 1839, this bird has had no less than eight different generic names. It has been described as resembling an overgrown warbler and as a "cross between a yellow-breasted chat and a chipping sparrow." It seems absurd that the green-tailed towhee is called a towhee at all. It is mostly because of its song that it remains classified as such. Its habit of scratching for weed seeds and insects beneath underbrush is a common activity. This same food is used to fill the gaping mouths of the young crowding in a nest on or near the ground in a clump of brush.

White-throated Sparrow

Zonotrichia albicollis

The chances of seeing this sparrow occur only during their migration to and from breeding grounds in the Canadian forest. This migration is also localized along the eastern edge of our Northern Rockies. Small flocks spend much of their time scratching on the ground creating such commotion in the dry leaves that each appears to be a much larger animal. Listening closely, a beautiful, cheery song sounds like "Old Sam Peabody, Peabody, Peabody," and indicates their presence. Any disturbance will send them fluttering out to an exposed perch, where again they sing the distinctive sweet song. The best identifying characteristics are the yellow lores and well defined white throat.

Male Red Crossbill 5½"
Green-tailed Towhee 6"

Male White-throated Sparrow 6"

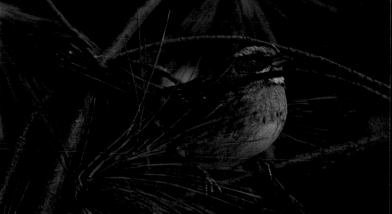

Savannah Sparrow
Passerculus sandwichensis

The first reported sighting of this sparrow was in Savannah, Georgia. Its range covers all of North America. The Savannah frequents margins of sloughs or marshes in low, moist, open areas. Because of its large range geographical variations in appearance are prevalent. If present, a yellow line over the eye is a good diagnostic characteristic. Its heavily streaked breast, short notched tail, and pale pink legs also help in identifying the Savannah. Seen mostly on the ground, seeds and insects comprise most of its diet.

White-crowned Sparrow
Zonotrichia leucophrys

The conspicuous head markings of a white-crowned make it an easy bird to identify. Frequently, when excited, the striking head feathers can be raised to form a low crest. With most of their feeding conducted on the ground, any startling threat of an intruder will scatter them into the nearest thicket. Here, they rely on their stillness and colors to go unnoticed. As soon as any real danger has passed they re-emerge to forage for weed seeds or spilled grain. In this same impenetrable vegetation used for protection, the female incubates her eggs in a small nest on the ground or lower portion of a bush.

Chipping Sparrow
Spizella passerina

A sharp chipping trill of the male during the nesting season is the call note from which this sparrow's name is derived. Very common along the edges of deciduous or mixed-wood forests, the chipping sparrow has also had little trouble adapting to human intrusion. Lawns and gardens in the country and in towns are their feeding grounds. They prefer to feed in the open, seeking insects and seeds. During nesting season they are largely insectivorous, thus supplying a good service in diminishing aphids, beetles, caterpillars, and other troublesome insects. In non-breeding seasons flocks of chippers wander through the woodlands nomadically, feeding in one area for several days and then suddenly disappearing.

Savannah Sparrow 5"
Male White-crowned Sparrow 6"

Chipping Sparrow 5"

Dark-eyed Junco

Junco hyemalis

Originally there was an Oregon junco and a slate-colored junco by classification. Both of these are known to hybridize freely and are now co-owners of the same scientific name *Junco hyemalis*. The slate-colored variety has a much larger range, covering the entire United States into Alaska, while the black hooded Oregon race is a western inhabitant. White outer tail feathers are the best identifying characteristic for the dark-eyed junco. Most of the year they are found in loose flocks, commonly feeding on the ground, chirping soft whispering notes. Weed seeds comprise most of their diet and they take readily to feeding stations. These flocks disband during breeding season. After mating, the male will assist in building a nest, takes no part in incubation, but assumes his share in feeding the young.

Fox Sparrow

Passerella iliaca

Secretive as they may be, these wary little sparrows are quite abundant in most parts of the Rockies. They inhabit dense brushy thickets, only emerging to forage on the ground. Even when migrating, they keep to the shrubbery and often go unnoticed. When searching the ground, they jump forward and back with both feet at once scratching among the leaves for insects and seeds. A summer harvest of ripe berries and other small fruits will also supplement their diet and the diet of their nestlings.

Dark-eyed Junco 5"   T. ULRICH
Dark-eyed Junco (Oregon) 5"   T. ULRICH

Fox Sparrow 6"   J. WASSINK

House Sparrow

Passer domesticus

Brought from England and introduced in New York about 1850, it took only 40 years for the house sparrow to establish itself in the Northwest. This adaptable small bird, which is not a sparrow at all, but a weaver finch, competes easily with the starling for being the most abundant and heartily detested bird. Very gregarious, it noisily feeds on seeds and grains found on the ground near houses or out in fields. It nests in crevices and corners of buildings, hollowed out trees, or occasionally makes a bulky stick nest in some tree branches. During winter, they frequent stations, feasting on seeds put out for more desirable species.

Lapland Longspur

Calcarius lapponicus

These longspurs are observed in the spring when they come migrating through on their way to nesting grounds in the far north. They travel in loose flocks alighting in fields to search for weed seeds. The male's breeding plumage is especially striking at this time. About mid-September, another influx of these birds passes through heading south, but this time they exhibit their dull fall plumage. Equally drab are the juveniles on their first migration. A characteristic long hind claw, from which they get their common name, is another excellent device to identify this group of birds.

Chestnut-collared Longspur

Calcarius ornatus

A typical bird of the dry short-grass prairies, the chestnut-collared longspur prefers land which has not been broken by the plough. Breeding grounds are remnants of virgin prairie, grazing lands, and dry grasslands, where on a weed stem the male will sing his pleasant song. Just below him, his mate is incubating on the ground, fully exposed yet blending in totally with the surroundings. The nest is simple, just a small depression lined with grasses. While raising her brood, much of her life is spent walking when foraging for insects or in short low flights to and from the feeding grounds.

House Sparrow 5"   T. ULRICH
Female Lapland Longspur   T. ULRICH

Male Lapland Longspur 6"   T. ULRICH
Male Chestnut-collared 5"   T. ULRICH

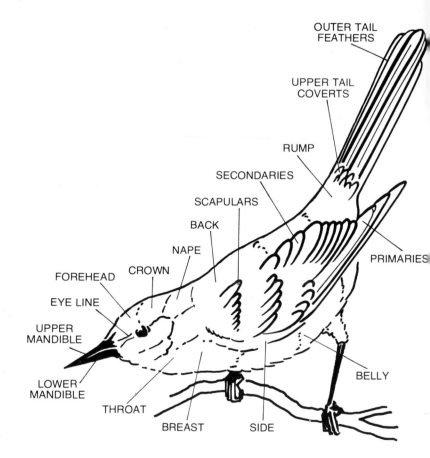

OUTER TAIL FEATHERS

UPPER TAIL COVERTS

RUMP

SECONDARIES

SCAPULARS

BACK

NAPE

CROWN

FOREHEAD

EYE LINE

UPPER MANDIBLE

LOWER MANDIBLE

THROAT

BREAST

SIDE

BELLY

PRIMARIES

Mike Ulrich

PARTS OF A BIRD

Glossary

Altricial — born blind, generally without feathers, and therefore helpless for some time after hatching.

Cambium — the layer of soft growing tissue between the bark and wood of trees and shrubs.

Carrion — dead and decaying flesh.

Clutch — a group of eggs laid by one bird.

Comb — a thick, usually red, fleshy piece on the top of the head on some birds.

Coniferous — trees that bear cones.

Crest — a tuft of elongated feathers on top of the head.

Crown — top of the head.

Dabbling — to feed by kicking in the water so head reaches for the bottom as rear end points skyward.

Deciduous — trees which shed leaves annually.

Dimorphic — existing in two different forms or colors.

Fauna — the animals of a given region.

Fledge — to become fully feathered and able to fly.

Gorget — a covering of brilliant feathers on the throat of male hummingbirds.

Gregarious — spending much of the time in flocks.

Hawking — to fly at or attack on the wing.

Indigenous — originating in the region where found.

Lek — a ceremonial piece of ground where some species of male birds, such as sharp-tailed grouse, gather to perform courtship displays to attract females.

Molt — to shed and replace feathers; usually after breeding and before fall migration.

Mustache — a colored streak of feathers running back from the base of the bill.

Nape — the back of the neck.

Nocturnal — active in the night.

Omnivorous — eating any kind of both animal and vegetable matter.

Plumage — the feathers of a bird.

Polygamous — having more than one mate at the same time.

Precocious — well developed at birth and able to run about.

Preen Gland — oil gland used when arranging the feathers to make them water repellant.

Primaries — the outermost and longest flight feathers of the wing.

Prolific — to produce offspring abundantly.

Raptors — a bird of prey such as a hawk or eagle.

Rump — the back portion of a bird at the base of the tail feathers.

Scapulars — a group of feathers on the shoulder of a bird, along the side of the back.

Species — a group of animals or plants exhibiting certain permanent characteristics in common.

Thermals — rising currents of natural hot air used by soaring birds.

Wing-coverts — small feathers that overlie and cover the bases of the large flight feathers.

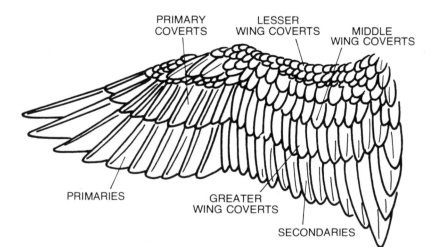

PRIMARY COVERTS · LESSER WING COVERTS · MIDDLE WING COVERTS · PRIMARIES · GREATER WING COVERTS · SECONDARIES

DUCK WING
Upper Surface

Mike Ulrich

154

Index

155

156

158

Notes

PRINTED IN TAIWAN